Trade and Environment

Contributions to Economics

Albrecht Ritschl
Prices and Production
- Elements of a System - Theoretic Perspective -
1989. 159 pp. Softcover DM 59,-
ISBN 3-7908-0429-0

Arnulf Grübler
The Rise and Fall of Infrastructures
- Dynamics of Evolution and Technological Change in Transport -
1990. 305 pp. Softcover DM 85,-
ISBN 3-7908-0479-7

Peter R. Haiss
Cultural Influences on Strategic Planning
1990. 188 pp. Softcover DM 65,-
ISBN 3-7908-0481-9

Manfred Kremer/Marion Weber (Eds.)
Transforming Economic Systems: The Case of Poland
1992. 179 pp. Softcover DM 69,-
ISBN 3-7908-91415-3

Marcel F. van Marion
Liberal Trade and Japan
1993. 298 pp. Softcover DM 90,-
ISBN 3-7908-0699-4

Michael Carlberg
Open Economy Dynamics
1993. 203 pp. Softcover DM 75,-
ISBN 3-7908-0708-7

Hans Schneeweiß/
Klaus F. Zimmermann (Eds.)
Studies in Applied Econometrics
1993. 238 pp. Softcover DM 85,-
ISBN 3-7908-0716-8

Gerhard Gehrig/Wladyslaw Welfe (Eds.)
Economies in Transition
1993. 292 pp. Softcover DM 90,-
ISBN 3-7908-0721-4

Alfred Franz/Carsten Stahmer (Eds)
Approaches to Environmental Accounting
1993. 542 pp. Softcover DM 178,-
ISBN 3-7908-0719-2

János Gács / Georg Winckler (Eds.)
International Trade and Restructuring in Eastern Europe
1994. 343 pp. Softcover DM 98,-
ISBN 3-7908-0759-1

Christoph M. Schneider
Research and Development Management: From the Soviet Union to Russia
1994. 253 pp. Softcover DM 85,-
ISBN 3-7908-0757-5

Valeria De Bonis
Stabilization Policy in an Exchange Rate Union
1994. 172 pp. Softcover DM 75,-
ISBN 3-7908-0789-3

Bernhard Böhm / Lionello F. Punzo (Eds.)
Economic Performance
1994. 323 pp. Softcover DM 98,-
ISBN 3-7908-0811-3

Karl W. Steininger

Trade and Environment

The Regulatory Controversy and a Theoretical and Empirical Assessment of Unilateral Environmental Action

With 12 Figures

Physica-Verlag
A Springer-Verlag Company

Series Editors
Werner A. Müller
Peter Schuster

Author
Dr. Karl W. Steininger
University of Graz
Department of Economics
Schubertstraße 6 A
A-8010 Graz, Austria

ISBN 978-3-7908-0814-8

Die Deutsche Bibliothek - CIP-Einheitsaufnahme
Steininger, Karl:
Trade and environment : The regulatory controversy and a
Theoretical and empirical assessment of unilateral environmental
action / Karl Steininger. - Heidelberg : Physica-Verl., 1994
(Contributions to economics)
ISBN 978-3-7908-0814-8 ISBN 978-3-642-49342-3 (eBook)
DOI 10.1007/978-3-642-49342-3

Softcover reprint of the hardcover 1st edition 1995

88/2202-5 4 3 2 1 0 – Printed on acid-free paper

Very few facts are able to tell their own story, without comments to bring out their meaning. In the case of any person whose judgement is really deserving of confidence, how has it become so? Because he has felt, that the only way in which a human being can make some approach to knowing the whole of a subject, is by hearing what can be said about it by persons of every variety of opinion, and studying all modes in which it can be looked at by every character of mind.

- John Stuart Mill

PREFACE

Even though the interlinkage between trade and environment is obvious and important, it has been acknowledged as such only recently by the world community. Yet it is far from being truly addressed, as is indicated by the negotiations up to the Uruguay Round Final Act, signed in April 1994, as the most current example. Mankind remains faced with the crucial need of addressing this interlinkage - the objective to which this report is devoted.

My own growing interest in this subject and the choice to work on and publish this report, which has been defended as my Ph.D. dissertation at the University of Vienna, has had a long personal history. Ultimately it was made possible by important teachers of mine - from primary and high school up to universities -, by colleagues and friends, but certainly also by my family - as each of them answered my questions and communicated their own ideas. Along the path of research it was only the specific support and inspiration of a large number of people in various different ways that made it possible for the report to now be in front of you in the current form.

My thesis advisors, Erich Streißler, through repeated hints on writing and in dialogues on the importance and place of the developments of economic theory with respect to my topic, as well as Stefan Schleicher, in numerous practical hints on getting over the rocky places of empirical research and through repeated encouragement at various difficult stages, have both contributed more than strongly by their scientific advice but also, and this I would like to point out here particularly, through their sustained personal support.

Lars Bergman offered his CGE model of the Swedish economy to form the basis of the current research and whenever setting up the Austrian model caused higher-scale difficulties he immediately granted advice. Fritz Breuss not only offered the most recent data basis he had developed, but also was a very careful discussion partner throughout the project. Karl Farmer helped to resolve my micro-economic dead ends, but most importantly gave support and numerous hints in accompanying me through the daily "ups" and "downs" of my work.

Throughout the research I profited from the comments and criticisms of my colleagues both at Graz and Vienna, Lutz Beinsen, Stephan Böhm, Egbert Dierker, Rudolf Dujmovits, Josef Falkinger, Ulrike Haslinger, Heinz Kurz, Christian Lager, Gerhard Orosel, Christian Schlögl, Erich Schwarz, Gunther Tichy and Gerhard Wohlfahrt. During a research stay, important information was supplied by George Akerlof, Michael Hanemann, Sherman Robinson and Silvia Weyerbrock at UC Berkeley, Ernst Lutz and Shanta Devarajan at the World Bank, Rodney Sobin and Carl Pasurka at the Environmental Protection Agency and Faye Duchin at New York University. Jacqueline Geoghegan and Jean Tesche supplied crucial hints for the empirical work throughout the project. Friedrich Mühlbauer, Johannes Potocnik and Elisabeth Vitztnum supplied immediate information on the Uruguay Round Final Act and Marrakesh decisions.

Especially within the final phase my colleagues at Graz enabled my dedication to this work by the way they shared our general university-responsibilities. My literature research was excellently supported by Elisabeth Colantonio and Doris Planitzer, and my English by Paul Miller.

But most of my debt I owe to my parents, to whom this work is to be dedicated, my brother and Ulrike Neier. Their strong encouragement and support in the daily steps towards the final results were the ultimate base without which this report would not have been written.

Graz, July 1994 Karl Steininger

CONTENTS

I

INTRODUCTION

οικειν

keeping house, managing, husbanding

How to use and especially share the use of resources is a focal question every human being and therefore mankind is continuously challenged with. Mankind´s history is one of steady efforts to develop and redefine the rule system governing resource access.

Simultanous demands and actions by a large multitude of individuals and communities at various levels have been smoothed by the framework of the economic and political order present in each period. The current framework that mankind has developed up to this, the last decade of our century, is to date crucially characterized by two main global challenges it has yet to meet. On them our main foreseeable focus will rest. First, the steadily increasing gap between the north and the south has been repeatedly addressed, but so far to a large degree unsuccessfully. Second, the recognition of ecological boundaries to human activities is of a younger age and therefore characterized by somewhat less experience. Within industrialized countries the main focus of political discussion is - due to its more immediate observation potential - on the latter; steps towards a solution of the environmental challenge, however, are very likely to also positively impact welfare in the developing world.

How is the use of environmental resources to be shared intertemporally among generations? How is it to be shared intratemporally among the multitude of potential demands? New rule systems for various levels (local, national, multinational and global) are in initial discussion. A common problem all of them face is their implementation potential being crucially determined by the non-autarky of regions. Interlinkages with other regions, nations or continents, can impede the introduction of any new "code of environmental conduct" considerably. Therefore, the preceding and more fundamental question is: What kind of rules should govern these interlinkages?

The questions that arise concern a framework that can ensure *sustainable conviviality*. How can the activities of a multitude of individuals and communitites be secured to remain within given ecological boundaries? How can these actors and acting bodies co-exist while the danger of them depleting their very life support system is diminished?

To explore steps towards sustainable conviviality and questions arising in its context is the theme of the present study.

For the full definition and also implementation of such a path, obviously, the combined effort of a broad range of scientists is required, demanding the contributions of political sciences, psychology, biology, theology, economics, history, linguistics and the arts, to name only a few. The present contribution can obviously only represent a part of such an effort, though one of substantial importance. Is it yet the *economic* interlinkages in our world that clearly can be considered to be among the most crucial. Arising from this importance, the particular focus of investigation is how the internationally economic interdependent system and environmental conduct relate to each other.

Both areas have strongly increased in importance rather recently. The growth in volumes of international trade is one of *the* central characteristics of economic development within our century, and especially characterizes the development since World War II.[1] In a parallel development within the last two decades, societies experienced a growing concern about the changing state of the environment, reflected in the introduction of environmental regulations.

Even though the obvious interlinkage between trade and environmental policies has been stated already at the 1972 United Nations Conference on Development and Environment (voicing that "environmental issues are going to exercise a growing influence on international economic relations"), the international community is only now discussing whether and how to address this interlinkage within legally binding frameworks.

To date, the discussion primarily revolves around the General Agreement on Tariffs and Trade (GATT), which dates from a period when the environment was hardly a concern, and therefore is not well equipped to deal with recent policy conflicts. One major question to be analyzed in this study is whether current trade regulation needs to bend to accomodate the new environmental laws or whether the danger of a protectionist misuse of such a regulatory change would be too severe to be tolerated.[2]

Current movements towards further trade liberalization pose the question of its impacts on the state of the environment. Does trade liberalization improve the environmental situation by enhancing allocative efficiency (of

[1] U.S. Congress (1992, p.3) cites one quantification estimate of this development: trade in manufactured goods to have increased nearly twentyfold since 1950, or two-and-a-half times faster than world output as a whole.

[2] Within the Uruguay Round trade negotiations this discussion was begun, but only a first set of environmentally relevant aspects is included in the core of the Final Act signed on April 15, 1994, in Marrakech (see section III.1.1. on GATT). With respect to most issues the discussion was put off the agenda and instead was acknowledged high priority in a next round of trade negotiations. To that end, in particular a finally agreed upon Committee within the newly established World Trade Organization (WTO) is to "identify the relationship between trade measures and environmental measures" and to "make appropriate recommendations on whether any modifications of the provisions of the multilateral trading system are required". The high priority of the issue can be seen in the fact that the Committe has already gone to work as Sub-Committee of the WTO-Preparatory Committee, with its first meeting held on May 11, 1994.

environmental resources), or is the growth effect it triggers dominating and detrimental to the environmental situation, when it is not sufficiently accompanied by a switch towards clean technologies?

Given a trade interdependent world, what effects does unilaterally stricter environmental policy have in open economies? How do short term, medium term and long run effects differ? Is it only worsening of the international competitive position that is caused or are there also substantial improvements in comparative advantage to be expected?

The latter set of questions, concerning unilaterally stricter environmental regulation, is particularly relevant for the case of Austria, which, being a small economy strongly dependent on international trade, simultanously experiences high levels of environmental regulation stringency. For example, the Institute for German Industry recently found Austria to be the country with the highest share of environmental expenditures in GDP among all OECD members.[3] Important aspects of the question will turn out to be primarily a matter of empirical quantification, which will therefore form a substantial part of the current investigation.

The study will start out in chapter II with a categorization of the various interlinkages present between trade and environment. The chapter informs on the matter of issues selected for further in-depth analysis and gives an overview of the remaining issues, also pointing out main references for them.

The first particular emphasis is to investigate the characteristics the international regulatory framework needs to contain to ensure mutual improvement of both the international division of labor and the state of the environment. This forms the question chapter III is devoted to. Starting with an analysis of the current regulatory framework (GATT, OECD Guiding Principles and EC law) it leads to the background question of

[3] UBA (1993), p. 33, with the most recent data available refering to 1991.

how, in the most basic terms, trade liberalization and environmental conduct relate to each other. This enables an evaluation of proposals for changes in the regulatory framework; proposals that currently are strongly growing in number, and often contradict each other.

One result of this analysis is that the current framework for most aspects allows countries to set unilaterally stricter environmental regulation. While there will be tendentious changes in the future, this basic feature of international regulation will remain. Countries do in fact evaluate the necessity for environmental regulation differently. Therefore there is discussion on setting stringency levels unilaterally more stringent. As this is legally permissible we can proceed to the second crucial question, that of the economic effects unilateral increases in environmental stringency imply. Chapter IV first applies theoretical frameworks to this question and in particular surveys recent results new trade theory supplies. Theoretical evaluation succeeds in pointing out what kind of effects are present. It, however, also points out that these effects often oppose each other. The importance of the individual effects is strongly dependent on the actual parameter values involved, such that many aspects of this question are actually ones of empirical quantification. Section 2 of chapter IV surveys empirical evidence gained in the international literature. Section 3 proceeds to empirical considerations for Austria, covering a determination of sectoral environmental control costs, an evaluation of international competitiveness of industries with strict environmental regulation and the particular case of the environmental goods and services industries.

Experience of past international empirical studies and these first statistical considerations for Austria set the criteria for the further analysis. They point out the most crucial question to be that of the effects of far reaching environmental policy (e.g. energy or carbon tax) on exposed industry sectors, and the importance of indirect effects of such policy. Both lead to the choice of the methodology computable general equilibrium (CGE) analysis to be used for the detailed empirical evaluation of this study, pursued in Chapter V.

As this empirical approach is - in international comparison - rather neglected in Austrian research, chapter V in section 1 first gives a detailed introduction to this methodology, its concepts, strengths and weaknesses. In particular the merits of this approach for environmental policy analysis are pointed out, also exemplified by a survey on recent environmental CGE modeling and its results. In section 2 the Austrian model is developed in terms of model structure, mathematical description and data base. The insights it supplies in policy simulations for unilateral environmental action are reported in section 3. The chapter closes with an evaluation of the approach and model application.

Chapter VI summarizes the main conclusions of the full study.

II

THE ISSUES OF INTERLINKAGE

Trade and environment issues are interwoven in various ways. Before entering into any analysis this chapter first categorizes the interlinkages. For illustration it also gives details of selected recent cases of international awareness.

At the outset the two main lines of influence can be separated: The question of how environmental regulations will affect both trade patterns and the gains from trade can be distinguished from the link running in the opposite direction; how changes in trade policy, in particular trade liberalization, will affect the state of the environment. This classification will prove helpful even though the effects are not fully unidirectional.

1. Environmental Regulation Affecting Trade Flows

For the analysis of environmental regulation affecting international trade flows it is helpful to distinguish three relevant modes of national environmental regulation:

Product regulations are established by the importing country and are designed to protect health and the environment in the country of consumption. They therefore may affect market access.

Production process regulations are designed to protect the environment of the country of production and may affect production costs and the international competitive position.[1]

A special subcase of the latter is that the method of *allocating the cost* of compliance with environmental process regulations may interfere with trade rules. For example, if pollution abatement equipment is subsidized by the government this may lead to charges of unfair export subsidies by trading partners.

The basic concern, from an environmental point of view, is that a regulatory international trade framework neglecting environmental concerns would prevent countries from the adoption of sensible environmental policies. Nationally independent product regulations could be forbidden by trade regulation (harmonization of product standards), or the introduction of process regulations could be feared to be accompanied by such strong effects of competitive disadvantage in a world of unconditional trade liberalization, that it is refrained from.

For the trade community the basic concern is that, if environmental considerations are given legitimacy in trade agreements, they may easily be misused as vehicles of new forms of protectionism.

Let us get into some exemplifying details of the different modes of regulation.

1.1. Product Regulation

The first category concerns the direct regulation of products.

> Environmentally related product standards are applied to products for the purpose of preventing environmental deterioration, or protecting consumers from direct environmental contamination.[2]

---

[1] As generally used in this study, the term "regulation" encompasses not only traditional command-and-control types of regulations but also market-based instruments. For

The most common types of this kind of standard relate to motor vehicle emissions, food products, toxic substance controls, product noise and packaging requirements. The country with the more stringent product regulation will find its competitive situation enhanced as imported goods which fail to meet the local standards are prohibited.

The most prominent European example is the Danish bottle case[3]. In 1981 Denmark passed regulation requiring beer, soft drinks and gaseous mineral waters to be marketed in Denmark in returnable containers; i.e., containers for which there was a system of collection and refilling under which a large proportion of containers used could be refilled. This effectively ruled out plastic or metal containers. Also, except for some limited circumstances, manufacturers could use only containers that the Danish Government had approved.

The Danish system is noteworthy because it went beyond mandating recycling of the containers' material to requiring reuse of the containers. The logistical and administrative burdens of such a system dictate that types of containers be kept to a minimum. That is why the Danish Government said it prohibited most use of nonapproved containers.

Foreign companies perceived these requirements as unfairly disadvantaging them because returning beverage containers for refilling would be more costly for them than for local producers. Moreover, requiring government approval for containers raised the issue of whether the Danish Government might limit its approval to a few standard bottle shapes, thus prohibiting foreign companies from using distinctive bottles carrying band recognition. The Danish regulation was also viewed with suspicion because it did not apply to milk and wine, two products for which Danish producers had little foreign competition.

---

production processes, this includes environmental taxes on inputs or emissions, for example.

[2] Pearson (1982) as cited in Dean (1992), p. 21.

[3] The overview of the case draws on U.S. Congress (1992), p. 89; an early reference is "Freedom to be Cleaner Than the Rest," The Economist, October 14, 1989.

The European Commission complained that the Danish regulation unduly restricted the free movement of goods among EC member countries contrary to Article 30 of the EC's Treaty of Rome. Initially, the Danish Government tried to mollify the Commission by amending its regulation in 1984 to allow the use of nonapproved containers (except metal) if volume was less than 300 000 liters per producer per annum or if the market was being tested and the new entrant provided a deposit-and-return system. However, the Commission continued to object, and in response the Danish Government argued that no further changes in the regulation were necessary and that the measure was justified by the need to protect the environment.

The European Court in its ruling in 1988 agreed with the Danish Government's position with regard to the deposit-and-return system for empty containers. It noted that protection of the environment is one of the EC's essential objectives, which may, as such, justify certain limitations to the free movement of goods. Responding to the Commission´s argument that there were less restrictive options available to the Danish Government, the court found that the burden of the Danish system was not disproportionate to its environmental benefits.

However, the court did find that requiring foreign manufacturers to use only government approved containers was disproportionate. Noting, that a system for returning nonapproved containers was capable of protecting the environment, the court observed that the volume of bottles at issue would be small in any case owing to the restrictive effect which the deposit-and-return system had on imports. It thus acknowledged that the restrictive effect of the measure would likely be substantial.

A way to minimize the development of any such conflicts obviously is the introduction of internationally harmonized standards. Initially, however, this only shifts the issue of conflict - towards the determination of the "right" level. An example: an initial GATT proposal regarding food safety harmonization was feared by a range of authors to establish an international standard on a level considered too low. In the course of the Uruguay Round, proposals have been put forward to recognize the Codex

Alimentarius Commission as a source of internationally binding standards for food safety.[4] This Codex Alimentarius Commission, which is jointly sponsered by two agencies of the United Nations, namely the Food and Agriculture Organization and the World Health Organization, so far only sets voluntary industry guidelines for food safety. Many authors point out that most countries' delegations to this commission have very heavy industry representation and much less environmental and consumer representation.[5] While these studies, in principle, consider the development of an international consensus on environmental and health standards to be a desirable goal, they fear that an enforced Codex Alimentarius would lead to a very weak international standard, and then tend also to operate as a ceiling rather than as a floor for environmental regulation. As the standards in the current Codex are less stringent than most developed countries´ existing national regulations (e.g. for the U.S. when compared to current standards of the Environmental Protection Agency (EPA) and Food and Drug Administration (FDA)), for the case of international enforcement of the Codex, it is often argued that such countries should be free to adhere to their own standards without being accused of being protectionist.[6] In the Uruguay Round Final Act a corresponding consensus has actually been established: the preamble of the Sanitary and Phytosanitary Agreement states that WTO members

> desire to further the use of harmonized sanitary and phytosanitary measures [...] on the basis of international standards, guidelines and recommendations developed by the relevant international organizations, including the Codex Alimentarius Commission, [...] without requiring mebers to change their appropriate level of protection of human, animal or plant life or health.[7]

---

[4] GATT Trade Negotiations Committee (1991), commonly "Dunkel draft", in its proposals on the Sanitary and Phytosanitary Standards (commonly SPS Code), p. L.46, paragraph 3.

[5] Arden- Clarke (1991), pp. 27-28; and as cited in U.S. Congress (1992): Wysham (1990), pp. 770-73; Hillard (1991), pp. 27-28.

[6] Dean (1992), p. 22; Arden-Clarke (1991), pp. 27-28.

[7] GATT Multilateral Trade Negotiations (1994), p. 69; see Annex A definitions, p. 77.

1.2. Production Process Regulation

The second area of country divergencies is that of regulating the *process of production*. Countries often will want to choose different levels of stringency in the pollution they allow related to production, the instruments being production standards or environmental levies of some form. As this affects the production cost structure, in this regulation category countries with stricter environmental regulations could experience loss in comparative advantage in the affected sectors. Furthermore, whole industries might relocate to countries with more lenient regulations.

It seems likely that in open economies environmental policy regarding production could involve a trade-off between the state of the national environment and the national share in international production. If this trade-off is quantified at significant levels, policy intervention may be called for.

Three options to mitigate competitive disadvantage effects are imaginable for countries with stricter environmental regulations. It could seek:

(1) to implement countervailing duties on countries with more lenient regulations. The argument would be that the lax standard can be seen as an unfair (nature-)subsidy,
(2) to implement domestic subsidies for environmental control costs, or
(3) to harmonize process standards across countries on an international level.

Let us begin with the last option, international harmonization. It is a very unlikely solution to be implemented on a broad basis.

On a fundamental theoretical level, countries differ in their environmental endowments as well as environmental preferences. The combination of the two will give the differences in national levels of environemntal qualities sought by individual countries. If production process harmonization is to standardize pollution per unit of output it could not acknowledge any relation to locally optimal policies. Most importantly, the basic reason for the benefit of trade, intercountry differences in endowments and preferences could not be taken advantage of.

If harmonization of process standards is understood to mean taking the preferred environmental quality level in each country as a reference level, it becomes a more than soft agreement. Countries would continue to define what meets their objectives best as "optimal", only then in light of the harmonization agreement. Also, it has to be noted, that neither of the two interpretations ensures equalization of environmental control costs (ECC), often stated to be the objective. Under the first kind of agreement ECC *may* be equalized for some countries, but the second is very unlikely to do this, not even for a few countries.

Aside from these theoretical considerations, implementation would entail a very high administrative demand - from setting the standards or tax rates up to international monitoring and dispute settlement.[8]

There is only one type of environmental problem for which the path of harmonizing production process regulation promises to be beneficial. It is global environmental problems, when countries agree on a targeted environmental quality level. Then this could be the clear reference point to evaluate production processes. The most evident example is the case of the greenhouse gas CO_2, namely to enforce internationally harmonized emission reduction regulation, e.g. by a harmonized CO_2-tax, as proposed by various country blocks.

When, however, there is disagreement on whether the environmental problem is or is not to at least some degree transnational or global, a clear conflict arises on whether foreign countries have or do not have a say in national production process regulation. This is the issue of extraterritoriality.

---

[8] For an evaluation of the harmonization approach in detail see Steininger (1994), also comparing the case of harmonization for product regulation, which is promising, with the one of process regulation in view in this section.

The recently most famous environment-and-trade case, the US-Mexican tuna case, belongs to this category of international disagreement. In the fall of 1990 the US banned imports of tuna from 5 countries (Mexico, Venezuela, Panama, Ecuador, and Vanuatu) because their fishing practices resulted in incidental dolphin killing significantly greater than the average for the U.S. fishing industry. The ban was grounded on the U.S. Marine Mammal Protection Act of 1988. Mexico subsequently called upon a GATT panel to review the US actions. In September 1991 the GATT dispute panel ruled in favor of Mexico, mainly on the grounds of GATT not permitting unilateral trade restrictions to protect the health of animals *outside the territory* of the country imposing the restriction, particularly since it did not involve an endangered species.[9]

The panel report, however, has not yet been adopted by the GATT Council, "and seems unlikely ever to be"[10]. Mexico, due to the politics of the North American Free Trade Agreement (NAFTA), has not formally sought its adoption, but also the United States could, under GATT's current practice, block the Council's adoption.[11] Other than these two directly involved countries, there is broad-based support for the tuna-case decision within the GATT Council, partly based on the legal principles involved, partly on its members being in opposition to the US Marine Mammal Protection Act practice themselves as it also requires an "intermediary nation" embargo of tuna from countries that do not act to prohibit their importation of tuna from countries under a "primary embargo" by the U.S. During 1992, twenty-two nations were hit by either the primary or intermediary embargo (for some time period). The tuna-case panel had ruled against the intermediary embargo as well, but this ruling has also been kept off the Council's agenda so far. After threatening to do so for several months, the EC filed a new complaint against the Marine Mammal Protection Act, which is currently pending before a GATT panel.

---

[9] Uimonen and Whalley (1994 forthcoming (fall), draft 1991), pp.22.
GATT panels, in similar cases also, always stated that they had no authority to rule on the *environmental* merits of the measures. See also section III.

[10] Charnovitz (1993), p. 37.

[11] see Charnovitz (1993), p. 38, and U.S. Congress (1992), p. 15.

This case has been a main catalyst to trigger broader discussion of several environmental issues in current GATT legislation and practice, also leading to new demands in the Uruguay Round.[12]

They also cover the other two options of mitigating competitive effects, countervailing duties or subsidies for national abatement equipment. These two options are more subtle than harmonization, and require the theoretical analysis of section III.2. We will return to them thereafter.

2. Trade Liberalization Affecting the State of the Environment

Current movements towards fewer and fewer trade barriers with the EC 92 internal market, the North American Free Trade Agreement, and also political efforts in South America and East Asia have granted high public awareness to the quantification of this link. The question phrased is, whether or not there is an unambiguous link between the removal of trade barriers and environmental degradation. On one hand it is argued that increased trade means increased production and use of resources and therefore a likely degradation of the environment. On the other hand trade might open the country to new and cleaner technology as well as improve the allocative efficiency with regard to environmental resources.

As the theoretical analysis of section III.2. will analyze in detail, the answer to the question of how trade liberalization affects the state of the environment depends crucially on the environmental policy implemented in the country(ies) examined. The assumed direct link between trade liberalization and the environment is complemented by an even more important indirect link via the parameter "environmental policy".

---

[12] See section III.1.1. (GATT) on the ultimately agreed upon Final Act and its environmental covering.

In graphic terms:

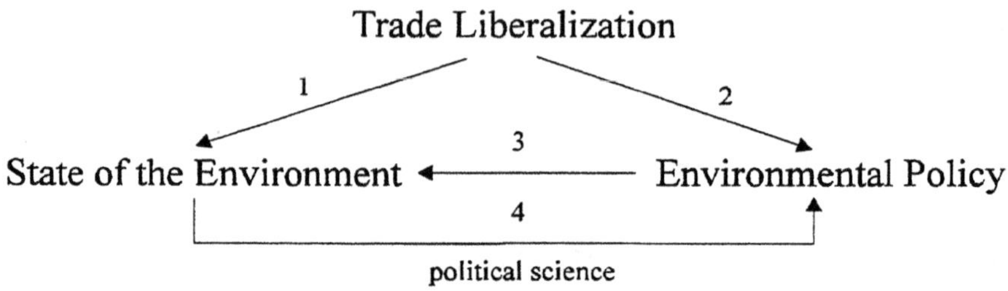

Trade liberalization will affect the composition of production (and thereby pollution) in the trading partner countries (LINK 1). The way this composition changes and affects the environmental quality depends strongly on the environmental policy implemented in the trading partner countries (LINK 2). Which environmental policies the individual countries will implement, however, also depends on the degree of openness of their economies and the environmental policy chosen by their trading partners (LINK 3). The state of the environment itself is a critical parameter in the process of environmental policy formation (LINK 4).

The last link mentioned belongs to the field of political science and shall therefore not be analyzed in this study. To restrain the scope further, link 2 can be seperated, dealing with the effectiveness of environmental policy and its various instruments in influencing the state of the environment. A good general overview on this latter issue is provided by Portney (1990). How the choice of the optimal environmental policy changes if we consider an open economy is studied by Krutilla (1991). In particular he focuses on the optimal level of an environmental tax. He points out that, in setting this level, the extra welfare effects of environmental policy via the changing terms of trade now have to be explicitely considered.

The current study shall focus on the two other links depicted in the above figure. The theoretical analysis[13] will deal with the combination of welfare effects due to trade liberalization and due to the changing state of the environment (link 1). For the question of what level of environmental

[13] Section III.2.

stringency countries that are open to the world market are likely to implement (link 3), the interesting issue is to analyze the effects of implementing stricter policy than trading partners have. To answer this question, first the international regulatory framework is investigated - where it stands and in which direction it is likely to develop - with the viewpoint of whether countries (under what agreements) are and will be allowed stricter environmental policy at all. Subsequently chapter IV analyzes the theoretical considerations and provides an overview of empirical studies. As the actual evaluation is mainly a question of quantification, an empirical study follows in chapter V, choosing the open economy of Austria as an exemplifying case of analysis.

3. Further Interlinkages

A range of further interlinkages between trade and environmental policies has partly already begun to evolve, but is rather more likely to develop in the future. Analytically, these issues are separate from those previously mentioned and go beyond the scope of detailed analysis in this study. Rather, the main points shall be presented in this introductory chapter and major references will be pointed out.

3.1. Trade Bans to Save Endangered Species

A variety of trade bans are currently in place already for conservation reasons. They are mainly based on the 1975 Convention on International Trade in Endangered Species of Wild Fauna and Flora (CITES), an international agreement whose purpose is to protect various wildlife species from extinction and overexploitation and makes extensive use of trade bans. CITES refers to two categories of species, either obligating parties to the convention to ban all commercial trade in the species, or, for the second category, requiring trade regulation through a permit system which countries themselves set up and administer. Compliance is voluntary and some parties, notably Japan in connection with certain species of whale and sea turtles, used GATT article XXIII (Nullification or Impairment) to exempt themselves from the CITES obligations.

The extent to which these trade bans are effective in conserving species has been highly discussed. The first analytical and empirical studies focused on a few key species. Barbier et al. (1990) concluded for the case of African elephants, that the trade ban encourages poaching and discourages conservation for two reasons. First, given the market demand for elephant products, the reduction in supply increases the price (in this case the black market price). Second, the prohibition on trade involves no property rights being allocated. Hence, poachers are given increased incentives to exploit the resource. Hence, they argue that responsible management of elephants as resources within a controlled trading environment, as opposed to a complete CITES ban, would provide a greater probability of resource conservation.

More recent studies, however, show evidence that for the particular case of elephant ivory the trade ban actually has been effective.

> Since 1989, when CITES enacted the ivory trade moratorium, elephant tusk prices have decreased from about US$ 100 per kilogram to between $2 and $3 per kilogram. Poaching has been reduced greatly and elephants have been observed to return to areas where poaching had previously occurred.[14]

Burgess (1991) expands the analysis of Barbier et al. (1990), relating data on international trade in wild plants and animals to extinction losses, and studying three more species in detail (parrots, wild cat skins and rhinoceros horn). Her conclusions support managed trade rather than complete bans.

> While over-exploitation of wildlife for international trade *generally* plays a minor role in species exctinction relative to other factors, particularly habitat destruction and domestic wildlife consumption, for a few species, international trade poses a major threat to their continued survival. [...] To ban all trade in a particular species, [however] may adversely affect domestic wildlife

[14] U.S. Congress (1992), p. 40, based on Pagel, Mark and Ruth Mace (1991), Keeping the Ivory Trade Banned, *Nature*, vol. 351, May 23, pp. 265-66 and on Aldous, Peter (1991), African Rift in Kyoto, Nature, vol. 354, November 21, pp. 175.

> management practices that rely on wildlife export revenues as a source of revenue.

A more comprehensive trade approach may be needed:

> A mechanism that allows a limited amount of exports from those countries whose populations are being sustainably managed offers an incentive to both consumers and producers to accept a controlled legal trade and enforce it. Using economic instruments such as taxes and subsidies to manage the trade could enable a larger share of the profits from the wildlife trade to be channelled back into the producer states to encourage wildlife conservation and support improved monitoring of harvesting and export activities.[15]

3.2. Trade Policy as an Enforcement Instrument for International Environmental Agreements

Policies to contribute to the global or regional transboundary commons typically involve a significant public good element, since one country's contribution confers benefits to all other countries. Therefore enforcement instruments play a crucial role in enhancing the incentive for individual countries to comply with international agreements. Punishment in the field of *environmental* repercussions, however, do not seem very plausible. A global carbon emission reduction treaty would hardly contain a penalty system allowing other countries to deviate from carbon emission reduction targets if particular countries did not meet their own committments. What seems more likely is that countries joining for this purpose will use the threat of trade actions in other non-environmental policy areas both to enforce environmental treaty committments and to penalize non-signatories seen as free-riding on the treaty obligations.

A first indication of this development is contained in the 1987 Montreal Protocol on Substances which Deplete the Ozone Layer. In its 1990 revision it requires the complete phase-out of CFCs by the year 2000. In article 4, it contains provisions applicable to *non*-signatories, but only relating to CFC-trade itself. Imports of CFCs from non-signatories are

[15] Burgess (1991), pp. 26-27

banned as of the beginning of 1990, exports to non-signatories are banned as of the beginning of 1993.

Uimonen and Whalley (1991) conclude that,

> [...] a global carbon reduction treaty, while still [...] far from being negotiated, may well have to confront [trade] issues of penalizing non-signatories to aid in compliance. Any trade actions which eventually result may well prove to be GATT incompatible.

They also mention a particular example:

> Thus, if concerns over global warming grow in profile over the next 10 or 15 years, pressures could be brought to bear on, say, China to reduce their coal burning in the form of trade sanctions. This could occur regardless of their consistency with international trade obligations, such as those under GATT (even though China is currently not a contracting party).[16]

Such trade threats are conceivable for all environmental matters; the connection will probably arise next with deforestation.

The concern of the trade policy community therefore is that the merits of trade policies one day might be no longer evaluated on their own rights, but primarily viewed as instruments to achieve environmental objectives, justified on the argument that this more than compensates for any trade losses.

A recent summary and evaluation of this issue is provided by Subramanian (1992). While he rejects all three kinds of interventions, direct trade interventions, supporting trade provisions and trade incentives (i.e. sanctions or incentives) based on environmental reasoning for almost all cases where they have been brought into discussion, he sees their potential merits exactly in the enforcement of environmental treaties, given that they have been multilaterally agreed upon. After summarizing all the cases where they should be refrained from, he concludes:

[16] Uimonen and Whalley (1991), pp. 9 and 36.

> However, the use of trade restrictive measures need not be entirely precluded: they might serve a useful rule in securing compliance with multilateral agreements or even in inducing 'true' free-riders to assume greater obligations. [..] Trade restrictions can be necessary or even desirable but only in [this] latter context, which allows truly cooperative solutions to be explored and secured.[17]

Also the "trade and environment" analysis released by the GATT secretariat (which can, however, not speak for GATT's members), while rejecting most trade measures for environmental reasons, states *this* issue similarly.[18] It therefore seems likely that international consensus can and will be found such that trade measures to encourage and ensure participation in international environmental agreements are considered appropriate.

3.3. Trade Implications of International Environmental Initiatives

Finally, international environmental initiatives will also affect trade flows between those countries that comply with them.

The currently most intensely researched area is the evaluation of potential effects of a Global Carbon Limitation Agreement. Here, the studies pursued in general point out that the effects on both country welfare and trade patterns depend crucially on the particular way the regulation system is constructed.

Whalley and Wigle (1991) analyze a carbon *tax* system with three possible schemes of revenue-redistribution, aiming at a 50% reduction in carbon emissions from what they would otherwise be. They use a computable general equilibrium framework to determine the effects on per capita

---

[17] Subramanian (1992), p. 151.

[18] GATT Secretariat (1992), p. 21: "It is often a challenge just to get a critical mass of countries - let alone all countries - to participate in an international environmental agreement. [..] Trade measures could be used as one type of 'carrot' or [..] as one type of 'stick' to encourage participation."

income (as a measure of welfare), which in turn effects trade flows. According to their results, developed countries would loose about 2.4 percent of the value of their income per year under a *global tax regime* (redistributing the revenues on a per-capita basis), whereas their loss would be significantly smaller (0.6 percent) under a (nationally administered) *consumption-based tax*. Developing countries lose about 4 percent of their income under a (nationally administered) *production-based tax*, whereas they gain 3 percent of their income under a global tax. Oil exporters obviously gain substantially from a nationally administered production-based tax, while they lose from either a global tax or a national consumption-based tax.

There are further regulation proposals, whose trade effects still need to be estimated empirically. Hoel (1992a) e.g. compares a tax system with a system of tradeable CO_2 quotas. He considers the latter to be much easier for the international community to accept mainly "as it looks more similar to the traditional agreements of the type 'uniform percent reductions'".[19]

For strongly diverse regions permit allocation obviuously has to be set up carefully so that it is acceptable to all potential participants. That it can actually be found is shown by Bohm and Larsen (1992) for the example of Europe and the former Soviet Union (FSU). While permit allocation by population, by GDP or some combination of the two is found hardly to induce participation by many Eastern European and FSU countries, they construct schemes that are both acceptable to Eastern Europe and FSU countries and still reduce costs for Western Europe relative to unilateral reductions only in Western Europe to reach a whole-region emission target. When Eastern European and FSU countries are, for example, allocated permits equal to their full projected emissions (and are thus overcompensated), they could realize significant net gains by reducing emissions until marginal costs of reductions equal the equilibrium permit

[19] Hoel (1992a), section 9. For the case of significant CO_2 reduction targets he, as most economists, also objects to the uniform reduction schemes arguing not only on the grounds of economic inefficiency, but also on the then only low incentive for sufficiently large participation, "since such a scheme gives a distribution of costs of reducing emissions which may differ strongly from the advantages the countries have from avoiding climatic changes."

price and then selling the excess permits to Western Europe. Western Europe would still save about 80% of the costs it would incur in the case of only unilateral reduction.

The financial transfers thus induced between East and West, and more so between North and South (by the initial assignment of rights), are, firstly, one of the most important elements of the global development strategy, and second, as a consequence will have strong effects on the volume and substance of future trade flows between country blocks.

Summing up, international environmental agreements are likely to have substantial effects on trade flows, the size and structure of which are most importantly dependent upon the actual inter-country financial transfers resulting from the agreements and, as such, re-determine international income distribution.

III

THE REGULATORY ISSUE

1. Current International Regulation

Out of the two areas of interlinking regulation, the one far further developed is obviously trade regulation. It is therefore also the most used point of departure for discussing the interlinkage. In this section we will look into the three main sources of trade regulation relevant for a European country, the General Agreement on Tariffs and Trade, the OECD Guiding Principles and European Community law, and their respective (potential) environmental coverage.

When approaching the issue from the reverse side, starting with a look into environmental regulation, many of the recent (multilateral) environmental agreements contain trade provisions. Out of the 127 multilateral environmental agreements valid in 1990, the GATT secretariat considers at least 17 to have such trade provisions[1]. Section II.3.2. has pointed out that the international community is likely to further employ this instrument to foster participation in international and multilateral environmental agreements - even in spite of possibly being found to violate *current* GATT regulation.

[1] GATT Secretariat (1992), p. 25, also supplies a table of respective coverage of current environmental agreements.

1.1. The General Agreement on Tariffs and Trade (GATT)

As the most important international trade regulation, our first focus is on the rules formulated in the framework of GATT. Dating back in its original design - in 1947 - to a period when the environment was hardly a concern, the GATT allows for environmental consideration only to a very limited degree. All "rounds" of further trade negotiations (with some exceptions in the most recent one) effectively did not change this picture. An indicator can be seen in the fact that the word "environment" does not appear anywhere in the core text of GATT until the Uruguay Round Final Act will be implemented. That this ommission remained was "in part because the main body of the agreement has been subject to very few ammendments, but also because the GATT focuses narrowly on the promotion of free trade", as Arden-Clarke summarized the development.[2]

Even though the issue also was not within the work program of the latest round of trade negotiations, the Uruguay Round (so-called for its inception at Punta del Este, Uruguay, in 1986) environmental concerns have come into limited discussion in its´ final phase since 1990/1991. A number of environmentally relevant changes are included in the Uruguay Round Final Act signed on April 15, 1994, to be discussed below. However, as the round has already been strongly delayed, most of the issues have been slated to be discussed and negotiated in a post-Uruguay Round.

An initiative launched by the EFTA countries had proposed a standing committee as the institutional setting for resolutions of future trade and environment questions, but the proposal was ultimately voted down, especially by the large developing countries. At the very completion of negotiations in December 1993 there was extensive discussion on work on this issue being a task of the World Trade Organisation (WTO), the newly created institutional framework for GATT. The compromise was to include this objective in the preamble of the WTO, which however is not

[2] Arden-Clarke (1991), p. 12.

legally binding. Nevertheless this is the first place where GATT explicitely covers the environment: [3]

> Agreement Establishing the World Trade Organization
>
> The Parties to this Agreement,
>
> Recognizing that their relations in the field of trade and economic endeavour should be conducted with a view to raising standards of living, ensuring full employment and a large and steadily growing volume of real income and effective demand, [...] *while allowing for the optimal use of the world's resources in accordance with the objective of sustainable development, seeking both to protect and preserve the environment* and enhance the means for doing so in a manner consistent with their respective needs and concerns at different levels of economic development,
>
> [...]
> Agree as follows:
> [...]

In the background of this discussion the practically more relevant changes with respect to the environment mentioned in the following subsections have been accepted.

In April 1994 at the Marrakech ministerial meeting to sign the Uruguay Round Final Act it was ultimately also decided to establish a Committee on Trade and Environment for the future work on the issue, though not as a negotiating forum, but to "identify the relationship between trade measures and environmental measures" and to "make appropriate recommendations on whether any modifications of the provisions of the multilateral trading system are required".[4] This committee can base its work in particular on that of the GATT working group on "Environmental Measures in International Trade" (EMIT), which was founded already in 1971, but convened in 1991 only - basically as the main sign of GATT starting discussion on the issue.[5] The "initial" work program for the new committee (to be reviewed at the first meeting of the General Council of

3 Uruguay Round Final Act, GATT Trade Negotiations Committee (1994a), p. 9; emphasis K.S.

4 Decision on Trade and Environment of April 14, 1994, GATT Trade Negotiations Committee (1994b); see also Appendix 1.

5 See pp. 31-32 for the convening and original 1971 mandate of the working group.

the WTO) is specified in more detail than that of EMIT was specified in 1991; the wording is supplied in Appendix 1.

The high priority of the issue for future GATT negotiations can be seen in the fact that the Committe on Trade and Environment has already gone to work as Sub-Committee of the WTO-Preparatory Committee, with its first meeting held on May 11, 1994.

1.1.1. Environmental Production Process Regulation and its Cost Allocation

There are basically three GATT principles that are relevant with respect to environmental production process regulation.

GATT Article I establishes the principle of "Most-Favoured-Nation" treatment, which entails that any trade advantage that a country grants to any other nation shall be accorded immediately and unconditionally to all contracting GATT parties. It thus prohibits importing countries from using import levies or taxes to discriminate between "like" products which, for reasons of differing *production methods*, vary in their impact on the environment.

Article III states the principle of non-discrimination, demanding equal treatment of domestic and imported goods. This principle, while intended to prevent Contracting Parties from raising the price of like imported products with an import tariff or levy, or by placing quotas or bans on these imports, in order to ensure free trade, also implies that an importing country cannot use such measures to safeguard the competitiveness of a domestic industry which has internalized more of its environmental costs than its trading partners.

If a country therefore seeks to avoid such a competitive disadvantage effect by covering the environmental regulation cost by means of a subsidy, this in turn is ruled out by Article XVI. This article requires that if a "subsidy operates directly or indirectly to increase exports of any product from, or to reduce imports of any product into, its territory", it must notify all other Contracting Parties of the subsidy. If any object, reduction or elimination of the subsidy must be discussed, on the basis that it may distort trade.

> This opens up any Contracting Party which subsidizes pollution control measures (for example), to a legal GATT challenge from any other Contracting Party with a competing industry which externalizes more of its pollution control costs.[6]

A range of authors sees the combination of these principles therefore to be in potential conflict with sound environmental policies, which most often optimally contain at least some ingredients of production process regulation.[7] As a first response and indicating potential further changes the Uruguay Round Final Act includes the provision that any subsidy for new investment due to environmental regulation of up to 20 per cent of investment cost is non-actionable, under the requirement that it

> is a one-time non-recurring measure; and does not cover the cost of replacing and operating the assisted investment, which must be fully born by firms; and is directly linked to and proportional to a firm´s planned reduction of nuisances and pollution, and does not cover any manufacturing cost savings which may be achieved; and is available to all firms which can adopt the new equipment and/or production process.[8]

1.1.2. Environmental Product Regulation

The structure and implementation of the case is different for environmental product regulation. Domestic regulation in general - not only environmental - can serve as a trade impedement. Especially since GATT Article XI prohibits (with some exceptions) any bans or restrictions on imports other than tariffs, countries, after tariffs and quotas had been substantially reduced in the seventies, soon created *domestic* regulations to impede imports in various more subtle ways. In the course of the Tokyo Round this triggered negotiations to reduce improper forms of protection

---

[6] Arden-Clarke (1991), p. 13.

[7] see e.g. Bown (1990), Arden-Clarke (1991), Shrybman (1991), Verbruggen (1991), U.S. Congress (1992).

[8] Uruguay Round Final Act, Agreement on Subsidies and Countervailing Measures, Article 8.2(c); GATT TNC (1994a), p. 239.

by means of the harmonization of technical regulations for products, laid down in a supplementary agreement to the GATT in 1979, the Agreement on Technical Barriers to Trade, popularly called the Standards Code. This Code, for our question in discussion, however, allows for exceptions for regulations that concern "the protection of human health or safety, animal or plant life or health, or the environment".[9] This means that for environmental product standards under this code countries *can* set them independently and tailored to their own circumstances.

To prevent divergent national standards creating unnecessary barriers to trade, the GATT secretariat must be informed in advance of the standards together with the test and certificate procedures. On the basis of this information the trading partners can evaluate the possible effects and make any relevant comments.[10] In case of urgency in regulatory actions only simultanous notification is required.[11] The code also provides for a procedure for the settlement of disputes.[12] While the core text of GATT did not include the word "environment", environmental regulation has thus been covered in the Standards Code already since 1979, but therefore with respect to product standard regulation only. Initially it was valid only for the signatories of the Code, of which there were 38 in 1993, about a third of the GATT contracting parties. By the Uruguay Round Final Act the Standards Code now is extended to all contracting parties.

The issue in product regulation already is that of how to decide on the proportionality between the trade-restricting effects and the legitimate objective of a proposed standard for the protection of health and the environment. Within the framework of the Uruguay Round, discussions were held on such a clearer definition of the Code. As a result the Final Act in the new Agreement on Sanitary and Phytosanitary Measures states the rules for a two-tier dispute settlement procedure with respect to measures to protect the health of human, animal and plant life[13], taking

---

9 Agreement on Technical Barriers to Trade, Article 2.2; GATT TNC (1994a), p. 118.

10 ibid. Article 2.9; GATT TNC (1994a), p. 119.

11 ibid. Article 2.10; GATT TNC (1994a); p. 119.

12 ibid. Article 14; GATT TNC (1994a); p. 130.

13 Agreement on the Application of Sanitary and Phytosanitary Measures, Article 2.1; GATT TNC (1994a), p. 70. Also the Sanitary and Phytosanitary Agreement

particular reference to scientific evidence. It is remarkably, that the reference level for proportionality has been ultimately lowered from "least trade restrictive" to "ensuring that measures are applied only to the extent necessary for protection".[14] In the foregoing discussion process on the proportionality issue many authors expressed their scepticism, especially as there was no earlier experience with dispute settlement within the Standards Code. Verbruggen (1991) states[15] that:

> [...] there are doubts about the feasibilty of such a thing as proportionality. No formal judgements are yet available on disputes arising from the Standards Code, so there is no basis as yet for the legitimacy of environmental standards as grounds for exemption from the rules.

Despite this lack of experience in definitive legitimacy, the Standards Code has been used to notify Contracting Partners. From 1980 through 1993, some 400 notifications under the code explicitely listed environmental protection as a justification of the standard.

The European Court decision on the Danish bottle case as covered in section II.1.1. is sometimes mentioned in this context as an example - to both ends. Some observers see it as highlighting how a court or other dispute settlement panel could apply a proportionality test to balance the competing but equally valid objectives of free trade. Others are critical of applying this kind of ruling further, stating that the court was too accepting of the national law, and that the decision could encourage other (in this case EC) nations to protect their industries with laws claimed to be necessary for the environment.

In this context it is noteworthy that this European Court ruling has never been challenged under GATT itself. It is, however, generally supposed it would stand were it challenged, though not based on an evaluation of its

therefore does not cover "environmental measures" themselves explicitely. However, the rules in handling the corresponding former exception XX(b) are now clearly specified in taking the exception into the core agreement. See section 1.1.3. on the interpretation whether "environmental measures" belong to this category of "measures to protect human, plant and animal life".

14 ibid. Article 2.2.

15 Verbruggen (1991), p. 689. Compare also a detailed list of difficulties in U.S. Congress (1992), p. 32 and pp. 59ff.

environmental merits, as would be demanded in a proportionality test, but because of its "national-treatment"-character. The European Court ruling actually remains one of the few cases where the panel explicitly weighed environmental merits and trade impedement effects. As was pointed out in the Mexican tuna case GATT panels never evaluated whether the environmental effect is beneficial.

1.1.3. Exceptions for Environmental Regulation in the GATT

Exceptions for environmental regulations are not only covered in the former supplementary Agreement on Technical Barriers to Trade that will become part of the core of GATT by the Uruguay Round implementation procedure, but may also be considered as being contained in the main text already. "May be", because interpretation of the respective passage is currently still under discussion.

GATT Article XX contains a number of specific grounds for exception to the general principles, subject, however, to the requirement "that such measures are not applied in a manner which would constitute a means of arbitrary or unjustifiable discrimination between countries where the same conditions prevail, or a disguised restriction on international trade". In particular, it allows for measures "necessary to protect human, animal or plant life or health" (XX(b)); and permits measures "relating to the conservation of exhaustible natural resources if such measures are made effective in conjunction with restrictions on domestic production and consumption" (XX(g)). These cited paragraphs do not explicitely mention environmentally related regulations, but the similarity of the issues makes them applicable and was called upon as justification in five environment-related trade restrictions so far.

To clarify whether these two paragraphs allowing for exceptions were already applicable to measures taken for environmental ends or whether the wording of Article XX(b) would need to be expanded to mention "measures necessary to protect the environment" explicitly, the EFTA countries under the initial initiative of Austria triggered an intense discussion process in both GATT and within the Uruguay Round negotiations on the General Agreement on Trade in Services (GATS). The Austrian initiative in May 1991 also was the reason for finally convening the GATT Working Group on Environmental Measures and International Trade, which had been created already in the context of the Stockholm Conference on the Human Environment in 1971, but had never been activated until the fall of 1991.[16] The work program of the group concerned the following: how trade provisions in international environmental agreements relate to GATT rules; the transparency of national environmental regulations with trade impacts; and the trade effects of labelling requirements for environmental purposes. Beginning July 1993 it was additionaly concerned with the follow-up process of the United Nations Conference on Environment and Development (UNCED). The original discussion on Article XX(b) and the correpsonding Article VIX of GATS, however, was not resolved until the (in effect: final) report of the chairman of the group was given in January 1994.[17] The work of the group now is continued in the form of the WTO-Preparatory-Sub-Committee on Trade and Environment.[18]

So far, the best picture of how the main body of GATT and environment currently relate is provided by the dispute settlement panel rulings interpreting these clauses when called upon in the five cases up to date, as mentioned above.

In the U.S.-Mexican tuna case as covered in Section II.1.2. the main issue was that of extraterritoriality when protecting the non-endangered species dolphins (otherwise covered under CITES), which the panel ruled down. In two further cases, a U.S. prohibition of tuna imports from Canada, and a Canadian requirement that certain salmon and herring be processed before export, the trade restraints were found to be unrelated to resource conservation. In the U.S.-Canada tuna case, claimed necessary for

[16] The mandate of the Working Group was "to examine *upon request* any specific matters relevant to the trade policy aspects of measures to control pollution and protect the environment especially with regard to the application of the provisions of the General Agreement taking into account the particular problems of developing countries", quoted from GATT Newsletter (1991), p.3.

[17] GATT Document L/7402, 2 February 1994

[18] Reiterer (1994) p. 10, footnote 9.

resource conservation under Article XX(g), the ban was rejected by the panel as it was not undertaken in conjection with a restriction on domestic production or consumption. In the herring/salmon case the GATT panel found that the Canadian restriction on unprocessed fish was not primarily aimed at conservation.

In a U.S.-Thailand cigarette dispute, a GATT panel found that the Thai import restriction was not "necessary", in that less trade-restrictive measures were available to protect health in Thailand.
Finally, a multi-issue case is that of Canada, Mexico and the EC complaining on the U.S. Superfund Amendments and Reauthorization Act of 1986 (its revenue to be used for the clean up of hazardous waste sites), which resulted in a higher tax rate on imported petroleum than on domestic, and a tax on certain imported substances produced or manufactured from chemicals that are taxable in the U.S. For the first issue the panel concluded that the tax differential between imported and domestic petroleum was indeed inconsistent with the national treatment obligation of Article II. As for the eligibility of the tax on chemicals for a border tax adjustment on downstream imports the EC claimed that OECD's polluter pays principle was hurt, under which such chemicals would need to be taxed in the home country. The panel, however, concluded that GATT tax adjustment rules are not concerned with the purpose of the tax (whether to generally raise revenue or to correct environmental problems or to serve some other purposes is considered irrelevant), the only important fact is that taxes are levied directly on the product. For downstream production, e.g. for imported products like perfumes containing the (U.S. taxable) substance alcohol, a charge may be imposed if it takes "into consideration the value of the alcohol and not the value of the perfume, that is to say the value of the content and not the value of the whole".[19]

---

[19] The GATT Panel citing an explanation of "equivalent" by GATT as the levying of charges equivalent to an internal tax imposed on a like domestic product is granted in Article II.
For matters of the Polluter Pays Principle, which is not contained in GATT, the panel reasoned that GATT does not contradict it, since a country is also free to charge a lower tax or none at all on imports when their production does not harm the

This implies that domestic environmental taxes under current GATT ruling can be charged equivalently also on imports (thus "levelling the playing field"), but only if they are levied directly on the product, and not if the domestic environmental tax is otherwise oriented, like charged on emissions or inputs. Even though for incentive, administrative or monitoring reasons such other forms of environmental taxes may be preferable, countries therefore might tend to rather shift towards product taxes. By this incentive to choose the potentially only second best instrument, current regulation fosters inefficient solutions to such environmental problems which arise in the production process rather than with the product itself.[20]

In a side ruling in the Superfund case it also became evident that current GATT inperpretation does not allow for any ad valorem penalties to force importing countries to provide information on the process and production methods employed, which some countries might seek, however, as the basis of counterbalancing measures.

Summarizing, the interpretation of potential exceptions by GATT dispute settlement panels, from an environmental point of view, has been very narrow. This is partly based, as the examples show, in the fact that GATT panels have never ruled on the environmental merits of any measures, because they considered this to be beyond their competence. Pearson and Repetto for example conclude from the five rulings surveyed above, that,

> [...] while the language of Article XX affords countries wide latitude in establishing environmentally-related product regulations, provided they are not arbitrary, discriminatory, or disguised protectionist measures, GATT dispute resolution panels and negotiators have attempted to narrow this latitude by interpreting exceptions (b) and (g)
>
> - to require that regulations impose the least burden on trade of all available regulatory measures [rather than using cost-benefit-criteria or proportionality-criteria, K.S.]

domestic environment versus higher charges on domestic products, which in the course of their production cause pollution of the domestic environment.
For a fully detailed review of these five cases see U.S. Congress (1992), pp. 81-90.

[20] Compare similarly Subramanian (1992), p. 143; and Sorsa (1992), p. 121.

> - to mean that a country's natural resources do not include a share of the global commons. [...]
> These interpretations seek to impose significant additional restrictions on the scope and autonomy of national environmental policies, in a decision apparatus in which environmental objectives and considerations are poorly represented.[21]

Conclusions from the other end of the spectrum, rather emphasizing the trade perspective, read differently as they accent different aspects. Petersmann (1992), for example, instead focuses on the rulings' emphasis on allowing for trade discrimination only when national production is equally regulated, this being in correspondence also with environmental economics.[22] This is correctly seen with respect to environmental economic theory, but not necessarily so - when sustainability aspects are given priority - with the political economic aspects involved, which, given the consequent impact on domestic industries, may give arguments for a (temporary) distinction between import and domestic practices to ensure sustainable resource use, especially in the case of developing countries. Arden-Clarke in this line uses the example of the forest protection in the Northwest of the U.S. to protect the habitat of the northern spotted owl. Limitation of timber cut was sought by export restrictions but there was unrestricted domestic use to secure supplies for the local industry and to maintain current employment levels in this region of the U.S. While this policy infringes the national treatment principle of GATT, Arden-Clarke considers it "necessary to make the limitation of timber cut politically and economically viable in this part of the U.S.".[23]

The second approval of current GATT regulation by the trade community voiced in Petersmanns evaluation concerns the denial of extraterritorial measures. This in fact is a crucial point of discussion, which will be covered below after the theoretical analysis.[24]

To sum up, the GATT (and the Agreement on Technical Barriers to Trade, popularly Standards Code more explicitly) grants countries wide

---

21 Pearson and Repetto (1991), pp. 18-19.
22 Petersmann (1992), pp. 260-262.
23 Arden-Clarke (1991), p. 14.
24 Section III.3.2.

latitude in environmental product regulation, but denies any trade measures in connection with environmental *process* regulation. Especially this latter circumstance is at the center of current discussion, also indicated by the fact that almost all environmental GATT dispute cases so far referred to this category of regulation. Negotiations in the course of the Uruguay Round therefore included proposals to extend policies allowed under the Standards Code for environmental product regulation to process and production methods also. After the theoretical analysis[25] we will go into the details of the diverging views on whether and how to extend policies allowed under the Standards Code also to a broader range of production and process standards.

1.2. The OECD Guiding Principles

The Organisation for Economic Co-operation and Development does not have the authority to change GATT or other trade and environmental agreements, but it offers a forum to 24 industrialized countries to discuss the issues. Comprising three quarters of world trade, in the past this group was by far the most dominant one in the wording of subsequent international trade regulations in the GATT framework. In contrast to GATT, the OECD has addressed the environment and trade issue already for some time, with "Guiding Principles Concerning the International Economic Aspects of Environmental Policies" adopted in 1972. In 1991, OECD initiated a series of member state discussions on trade and environmental issues, jointly supported by its two Trade and Environment Directorates. This process, in theory, could produce guidelines for application by OECD member states. Though an attempt is being made to also consider developing countries concerns, the absence of developing countries from OECD membership, however, is a major limitation that is unlikely to be overcome by the observer status given to Mexico and a few Eastern European countries. The new guidelines were initially expected to be ready for adoption at the June 1992 Ministerial, but in spite of specific progress made have not been adopted as of July 1994.

---

[25] Section III.2.

As the OECD is the main group also framing GATT and dispute settlements, the baseline of the 1972 Guiding Principles is mostly in concordance with the one given above in the section on GATT, though with much more explicit reference to environmental matters. While therefore many environmental aspects are adressed more fully, OECD states only principles and does not provide any dispute settlement mechanisms, which limits the guidelines application. OECD put forward four principles:[26]

1. Polluter Pays Principle: If national authorities consider a regulation necessary to protect the environment, then polluters should bear the costs of satisfying that regulation. The guideline allows exceptions, particularly for transitions, that do not greatly distort international trade and investment. As subsequently interpreted, the departures might include government help (in exceptional circumstances) to address socio-economic problems arising from rapid implementation. Aid to stimulate experimentation with new pollution-control technologies and development of new pollution abatement equipment would not necessarily be incompatible with the polluter-pays principle.

2. Harmonization Principle: While stating reasons that justify differences in national environmental policies (mainly differences in assimilative capacities, social priorities, degrees of industrialization, and population density), the principle emphasizes at the same time the government's task to seek harmonization of environmental policies, where valid reasons for differences do not exist.

3. National Treatment and Non-discrimination: Reference to the GATT principles is made.

4. Compensating Import Levies and Export Rebates Principle: When harmonization of standards is not achieved, in any case "differences in

---

[26] The overview is based on OECD Secretariat Notes for the Joint Sessions of Trade and Environment Experts, the first session held October 1, 1991; and U.S. Congress (1992), p. 26; in the German literature they are surveyed for example by Petersmann (1992), pp. 264-265.

environmental policies should not lead to compensating import levies or export rebates (border adjustments) or measures having an equivalent effect, designed to effect the consequences of these differences in prices."

The last principle is in line with GATT and GATT dispute panel ruling, though, as the Superfund Case showed, it can be circumvented, when the form of product taxes is chosen as an instrument to address an environmental problem.[27]

Comparing the OECD guideline to GATT regulations, subsidies for environmental regulation are here allowed to a limited degree (for the transitional phase). Within GATT subsidies will only be allowed with the implementation of the Uruguay Round Final Act, restricted to 20% of the full investment cost due to new environmental regulation and on a one-time-basis. For border adjustment measures the issue of discussion is the same as under GATT as covered above, the OECD also not allowing them for any environmental control cost compensation reasons.

The currently active discussion process, while regarding these principles as being generally and continuously valid, was initiated to develop guidelines for further areas: trade measures in international environmental agreements; effects of trade policies on the environment; and application to developing countries. In the 1993/94 session the main focus of the working group was rather on how the trade framework should relate to national environmental process and production methods regulation.

1.3. European Community Legislation

Similarly as with the GATT, conflicts have also arisen within the European Community between the objective of trade liberalization and given competences of environmental regulation. One major distinction to GATT is the absence of a law comparable to the "national treatment clause" in GATT. Therefore national environmental regulation, that would not be considered as a trade restriction under GATT Article III,

[27] Compare section III.1.3 above.

could be in contradiction to Article 30 of the Treaty of Rome that forbids any measures restricting the free movement of goods among EC member countries.[28]

This conflict was first resolved in the course of the Danish bottle case[29], where the European Court weighed between the objectives of free trade (Article 30) and environmental protection (Articles 36, 100a, 130r-t) and concluded that environmental protection is a "compulsory objective of Community Law" that may justify the restriction of trade. If there is no Community regulation and the national measure is non-discriminating, necessary and proportionate, than it cannot be considered as trade restriction in the sense of Article 30. This ruling confined Article 30 in the sense of GATT Article III, with the additional requirement of necessity and proportionality, the determination of which under GATT is left to the individual Contracting Parties. However, also for GATT, in the course of the Uruguay Round negotiations on the Standards Code (and the newly established Sanitary/Phytosanitary Code) there have been similar proposals for the testability of necessity and proportionality of technical restrictions and requirements,[30] including those processing methods that are intended to render a product "fit for use".[31]

The most important difference in European Community regulation compared to GATT regulation, however, is the large number of common environmental regulations. The EC has adopted nearly 300 directives and regulations specifically concerned with the environment.[32] Pearson and Repetto additionally point out that these regulations have tended to be harmonized at relatively stringent levels.[33] Similarly to GATT, countries are allowed to individually implement individually more stringent levels, but generally not lower ones. In the Maastricht Treaty, the possibility of

---

28 Under the classical "Dassonville definition" "any measure that qualifies to hinder inner-community trade directly or indirectly, actually or potentially" has to be considered as a "measure of equal effect" forbidden under Article 30, Rs 8/74, Dassonville, EuGHE 1974, p. 837; as cited in Petersmann (1992), p. 265.

29 See section II.1.1.

30 See Petersmann (1992), p. 266.

31 See Gavin (1992), p. 79.

32 U.S. Congress (1992), p. 20.

33 Pearson and Repetto (1991), pp. 11-12.

temporary exceptions allowing for lower standards is also covered, if the common regulation would "imply unproportionally high costs for the authorities of a member country"[34]. Then also technical assistance and financial support can be provided for those originally weak-standard countries. For the allowance of more stringent standards, however, a distinction between product and process regulation applies. For product regulation more stringent levels are permitted only when taken for non-economic, environmental reasons. For process standards the regulation´s motivation is usually not an issue.

Aside from this specific effect of the distinction, it is interesting that this distinction between product and process standards also marked the breakthrough within the general EC environmental regulation. The original treaty dated to the fifties and therefore did not contain environmental considerations. In 1973 the "first environmental action programme" was launched, but there was no special competence. As the basis for all common environmental regulation two very general Articles had to be used: Article 100, stating the common market objective, and Article 235, stating that when there is no competence of the EC, but measures were necessary for the functioning of the Community, they could be taken. This implied that consensus was necessary among all members on any new common environmental regulation, leading to very few decisions already before the south-extension was accomplished, even though northern countries are generally considered to be more homogenous in environmental respects.

When the EC was joined by the southern countries Spain and Portugal in 1986, the legal treatment of environmental regulation was differentiated depending on whether it concerned product or process regulation. Product regulation is now covered under Article 100a, necessitating only a "qualified" majority. In practice this means that neither all the big countries nor all the small countries alone could gain a majority for environmental product regulation. As such the common market can be better fostered than with full consensus-requirement while clear

---

[34] Petersmann (1992), p. 266, own translation.

protectionism is nevertheless forestalled. For process regulation, now covered under Article 130s, a consensus among all members is still required such that poorer countries cannot be voted down in their preferences for (usually lower) environmental quality levels. In practice, this, however, has led to a current persistent hindering of new environmental process regulations, mainly by Spain[35].

The almost 300 directives passed meanwhile nevertheless point out the progress in EC common environmental regulation, though it has to be noted at the same time, and this is the weak point in current EC environmental regulation, that member countries often have been very slow to implement them or have even ignored them. As of early 1990, for example, the European Commission had identified 303 cases in which member nations had incorrectly or incompletely implemented EC environmental directives.[36] So, also in various cases of common regulation, some countries effectively have unilaterally more stringent standards than the slow-implementing ones. But overall, the EC has had to and has addressed the environment-and-trade issue more directly than the rest of the world.

2. Theoretical Background

2.1. The Effects of Trade Liberalization on the Environment

At the root of the concern whether the current trade regulatory system is threatening to or supportive of environmental improvement lies the question of how international trade in general affects the environmental situation.

---

[35] Johannes Mayer, Austrian Chamber of Commerce, and member of the OECD Group of Environmental and Trade Experts 1991/1992, oral information in the course of a talk at the Austrian Interuniversitary Research Institute, 17 November 1992.
For a comprehensive overview on EC environmental regulation see for example Keyes (1991).

[36] French (1991), pp. 26-33.

Let us give the baseline answer to this question in the framework of a simple standard two-commodity international trade diagramatic analysis. It is assumed that only two countries exist, country A (the home country) and country B (the rest of the world), that transport costs are absent and that perfect competition prevails in international markets. Both countries use the same factors which are internationally immobile and produce the same goods.

In the absence of trade both countries will be in a situation of equilibrium, each having a relative price ratio between good 1 (the environmentally relevant good) and good 2 (all other goods) and simultanously the respective produced quantities are determined.

For any of the reasons that explain the emergence of trade among countries - different productivity (or technology) (Ricardo), different factor endowment (Heckscher-Ohlin), increasing returns to scale (Krugman) or, on the demand side, differences in tastes among countries - it is very unlikely that the autarky equilibrium price ratio is the same in both countries. Let us assume that it is not and without loss of generality further assume that this ratio is greater in country A than in country B, as shown in Figure 3.1. This back-to-back diagram shows the supply and demand curves for the same commodity 1 for both countries, they determine the respective autarky equilibrium price ratios.

When trade is opened up the (world market) international price ratio will lie in between the two internal equilibrium price ratios. The world price ratio will take such a value that the quantities sold on world markets match in size. i.e. the international equilibrium is established at a point where the excess supply of good 1 by country A (country A's supply of exports) is exactly matched by the excess demand of the same commodity by country B (country B's demand for imports).[37] The opening up to trade therefore implies a shift in production; country A increases production of good 1 and decreases production of good 2. The comparative advantage in country B is the reverse.

[37] For further characteristics of this model reference can be made to any standard textbook on international economics, e.g. Gandolfo (1987), chapter 3.

Figure 3.1: Determination of International Equilibrium

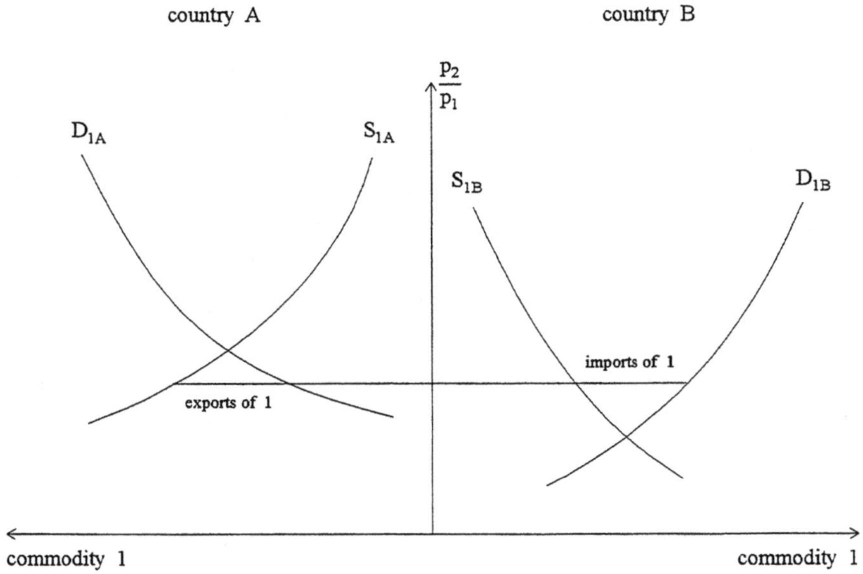

When specifying the environmental characteristics of the model we can determine the environmental effects of trade. We assume that only production externalities shall be present and without loss of generality further assume that they occur at the production of the good (or the goods summarized by) 1. There shall also be no transfrontier pollution arising from this production externality.

The shift of production of good 1 towards country A then implies a pollution increase in country A and a decrease in country B. How can this be evaluated? Most will agree that there is no naturally given, "subjectively" optimal pollution level, that mankind could easily recognize. Most importantly, earth´s history with changing levels of natural pollution does not supply us with such a level. What the natural sciences supply us with is the scope of the range of geogenic flows. A most broadly accepted criterium for sustainability is the request to keep the amount of human flows such that this geogenic range is not exceeded.[38] Sciences also point out the (sometimes large) absorption capacity of ecological systems, but also that for each system there exists a not exactly predictable level of excess load (depending on a range of factors), where the system tips over. Societies currently seem to be recognizing more and more areas where mankind has exceeded this level. Our point here is that for an evaluation of pollution levels, a judgement is necessary that cannot take recourse to any "naturally given" optimal level, and that mankind cannot do anything other than to formulate such a judgement itself - to the best of its knowledge.[39] For finding a "best level" almost nobody would request that all pollution due to human production needs to be stopped, as this would end almost all production activities. Rather, society seeks to find the right balance between production and a preferred (or even for its survival necessary) environmental quality level.

Not going into the details of discussing the methods e.g. of environmental economics in determining this balance and into the political processes of finding consensus and implementing it, the point for this first basic theoretical analysis is only that in principle, society could find such an optimal balance between the benefits of environmental quality and the benefits of goods and services produced (or, rather, the amount of effort needed to produce them according to the production process chosen). This balance is exactly what is meant by the often called for 'fully internalizing (governmental) policy'. For the theoretical approach it shall serve as our reference level[40].

When governments implement such a first-best national environmental policy in both counries, internalizing pollution effects coupled with the production of good 1, and assuming that it would be binding, this would

[38] Compare for example the definitory chapter 2 of SUSTAIN(1994).

[39] That in some areas this may also involve countering delayed environmental problem recognition is shown in an economic analysis of the effects of illusion in Steininger (1993).

[40] A further assumption necessary for the analysis chosen is that the income elasticity of each good is independent of the amount of the other good consumed. Otherwise the welfare analysis for production shifts of commodity 1 would have to include considerations on the quantity changes of commodity 2. This, however is a standard assumption in economic welfare analysis. For exposition see e.g. Layard and Walters (1978) pp. 33.

Figure 3.2: Environmental Policy Shifting the Supply Curve

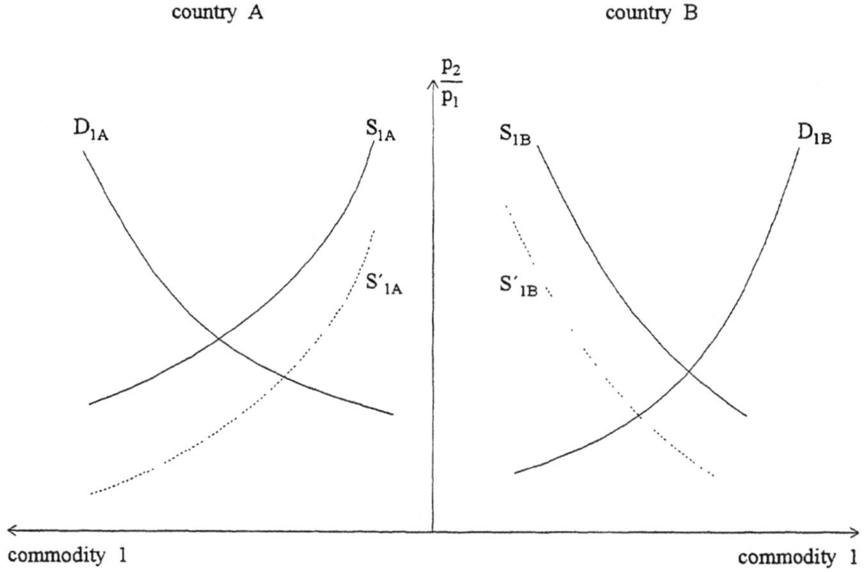

shift the supply curves downwards in the diagramatic analysis (the broken curves S_{1i}' in Figure 3.2), as for any relative output price ratio of the two goods, less of commodity 1 will now be produced. The reason being that production costs for the firms, who now have to bear the environmental costs themselves, will have gone up. In other words, the supply curves are the sum of all producers marginal cost curves, which have shifted upwards due to the environmental regulation, such that the same quantity of commodity 1 is now only sold at a much higher price p_1, i.e. at a lower price ratio p_2/p_1.

In Appendix 2 the shift of the general equilibrium supply curve is derived more rigorously from the shift in the production possibility frontier caused by environmental policy.

This gives us the instrumentarium at hand to determine the effects of trade liberalization distinguishing the two cases of (1) when national fully internalizing environmental policy is implemented and (2) when such a policy is not (or not sufficiently) implemented.

2.1.1. National Environmental Policy Set Sufficiently

While in autarky, countries would produce at point X depicted in Figure 3.3, international trade shifts production towards Y in installing a new international relative price p_2/p_1. As we can take for granted that due to the chosen national environmental policy, benefits from production and environmental quality are already weighed optimally, we can immediately draw conclusions on the overall net welfare effect for society due to international trade. Similarly as with national division of labor, both countries incur a welfare gain based on their comparative advantages. Country A will export good 1, whose relative price has increased (p2/p1 is lower than in autarky), and therefore can afford a higher real consumption level (mainly the now imported good 2 is cheaper than when it would have been when produced at home). The welfare gain can be graphically depicted by the change in the relative price compared to singular production possibility and demand preferences, the shaded triangle XYZ_A in Figure 3.3.

Figure 3.3: Welfare Gain When Environmental Policy is Set Sufficiently

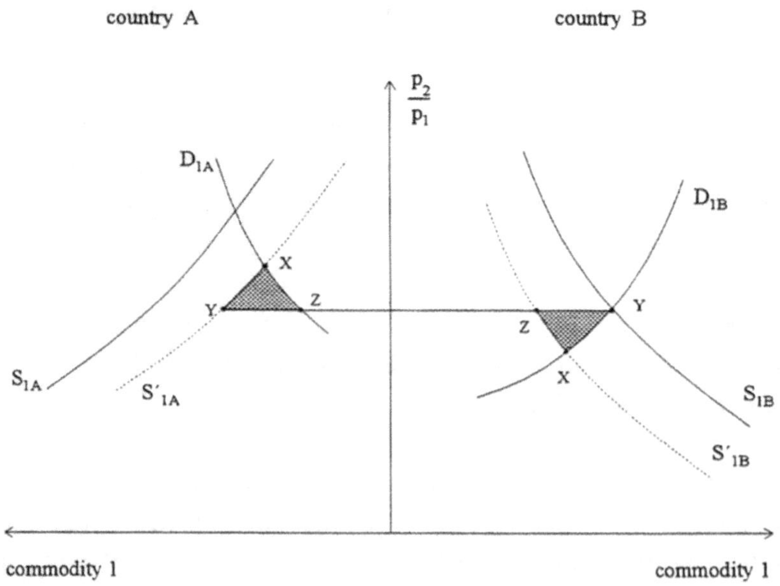

Similarly, country B, an exporter of commodity 2, the relative price of which has improved compared to *its* autarky level, incurs a gain of trade depicted by the triangle XYZ_B.

2.1.2. National Environmental Policy Set Insufficiently

Let us for the moment additionally assume that the countries are small relative to the world market, so that they have no influence on the world market price. In other words, p2/p1 is given independent of individual country policy.

With - at the extreme - no environmental policy at all, then, for the country exporting the environment-intensive commodity, the increased production of it (the increase now is greater than in the above case) causes welfare losses. They can be measured by the difference of private and social costs (the external environmental damage) incured for each unit of production, the rectangle TUVW depicted in Figure 3.4. Now, turning to the benefits of trade, a measure of gains to trade that is insensitive to environmental change (let us call it traditional gains from trade TUZ) may or may not be outweighed by this welfare loss due to increased pollution.

For the importing country, whose situation is given in Figure 3.5, the reduction of the pollution-intensive production translates into an additonal environmental welfare improvement TUVW, that adds to the tradional gains to trade measure TUZ.

For relaxing the small country assumption, the effects are somewhat more complex as the introduction of environmental policy in one country also effects the welfare in the other country(ies) via changing p2/p1, i.e. changing the terms of trade. But the underlying reasoning remains the same.

If the pollution is related to consumption of the product and not to production, obviously the reasoning is reversed, the importing country now worsening its welfare situation when it doesn't regulate the use of the product sufficiently.

Figure 3.4: Welfare Effects for the Country Exporting the Environmentally Intensive Good

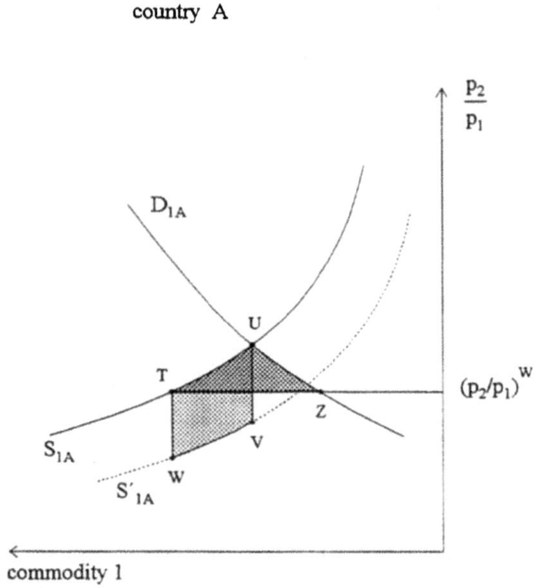

Figure 3.5: Welfare Effects for the Country Importing the Environmentally Intensive Good

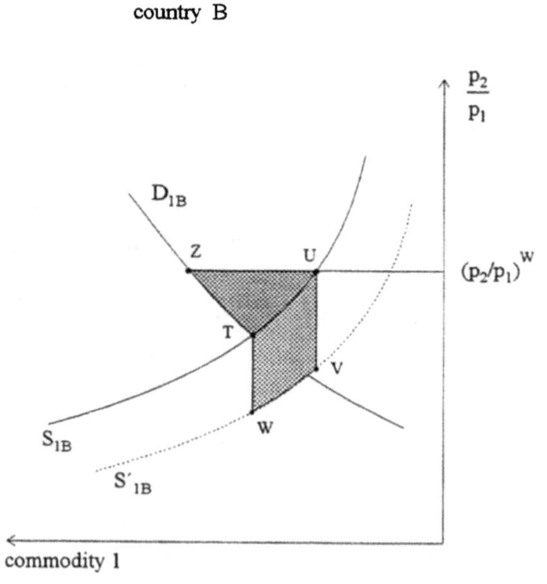

Figure 3.6: Net Environmental Effect of Lifting Trade Barriers When Environmental Policy is Set Insufficiently

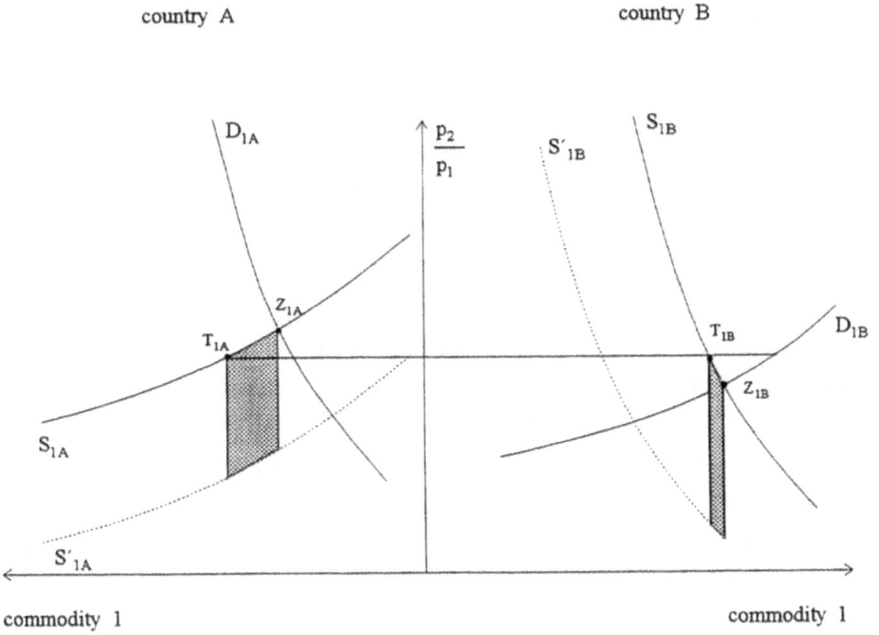

If one seeks to evaluate the net purely environmental effect aggregated over both countries, adding up the benefits of reduced pollution in one country and the losses of increased external costs in the other country might - with limitations - be considered as representing such a measure.[41] The net overall environmental effect of liberalizing trade then depends upon (a) the relative slope of the demand and supply curves in the two countries and (b) the relative size of environmental externalities in both countries. For example, for a situation as depicted in Figure 3.6, where the supply curve in the country with the comparative advantage in the pollution intensive commodity is relatively flat, and the demand curve is steep,[42] versus a contrary situation in the other country(ies), namely a

[41] The limitations are clearly nonlinearities and synergy effects in environmental damage not considered by such a simple addition.

[42] The slope of the general equilibrium supply curve represents the change of the marginal rate of transformation between the two commodities along the production possibility frontier, which can be easily seen in Figures A.1 and A.2 in the appendix. A flat supply curve implies that production can be changed easily to substitute

steep supply and flat demand curve, the net environmental effect tends to be negative. This could be counterbalanced only by a large divergency in the second decisive parameter - namely a much larger negative environmental effect per unit of production in country B relative to hardly any environmental damage per unit of production in country A. In the diagram the distance of S_{1B}' to S_{1B} would have to be much larger than the distance of S_{1A}' to S_{1A}. This measuring applies, to note it again, when national environmental policy is set insufficiently.

2.1.3. Conclusion

International trade most likely causes changes in national pollution intensities. But, where a fully internalizing environmental policy is implemented, production levels are chosen such that they ensure net welfare gains for all participating countries. If, however, environmental policy is for any reason set insufficiently, in some countries the environmental situation will worsen such that it may even outweigh other benefits from trade for these countries.

The international market, like any other market, does not correct for any market failures, including environmental externalities. But, on the other hand, international trade is generally not the basic cause for potential environmental degradation, the root cause usually is domestic environmental conduct. What trade typically can do is to magnify the effects of domestic conduct. That is why trade barriers so far have often served as unintended environmental safeguards - namely in those cases where national environmental policy was set insufficiently.

---

towards commodity A (diagramatically a flat and stretched production possiblity frontier).

The slope of the respective demand curve represents the change in the marginal rate of substitution along the social indifference curve. A steep demand curve implies that substitution towards commodity A is highly inelastic.

2.2. Evaluating Trade Measures for Environmental Ends

The baseline argumentation arising from the last section is that environmental problems are best solved by addressing them directly. Trade restrictions, while having an effect on the environmental situation, simultanously have further reaching (distorting) effects preventing society from achieving international division-of-labor welfare gains. Any trade restriction, be it for environmental purposes or other purposes, always also involves welfare losses.

Trade measures for environmental purposes, viewed in this perspective, should therefore only be taken if they are very close to the root of the environmental problem, and thus solve the environmental problem without other large distorting effects. What "very close" means, depends first on the characteristics of the environmental problem, mainly the geographic scope, but, second, will also be seen differently according to the paradigmatic background this evaluation is drawn from as section 3 will subsequently point out.

2.2.1. Cases where Trade Strongly Contributes to the Environmental Problem

One example in this category, where trade is close to the root of the environmental problem, is the disposal of hazardous waste. Accordingly, the Basel Convention on the Control of Transboundary Movements of Hazardous Wastes and their Disposal bans export of hazardous waste where improper disposal would appear to be likely, e.g., wastes sent to countries lacking adequate regulations or the technical capacity for proper disposal.

More controversial is the case of trade in tropical timber.[43] GATT Secretariat (1992), to name the exponent of one view, considers, for example, an often requested trade ban to have little potential effect on tropical forest conservation, because over 80 percent of tree cutting in developing countries is due to fuel wood harvesting and land-clearing for

[43] The overview given draws partly on U.S. Congress (1992), p. 43.

agriculture and ranching, while tropical timber exports account for only 1 percent of trees felled in developing countries.[44] Proponents of tropical timber trade restrictions - who are not all proponents of trade bans - counter by noting that some countries are much more affected by export timber demand than aggregate statistics suggest. Malaysia and Indonesia account for over 75 percent of tropical timber exports[45], certain land forms are more vulnerable to damage from logging than others, and commercial logging operations catalyze agricultural land-clearing by making new forest areas accessible to settlement. Suggestions by such proponents often include, similar to the case of endangered species,[46] limiting imports to producers that can certify their use of sustainable forest management techniques, as this would increase the value of sustainably harvested tropical timber and thus increase incentives for conservation.[47]

2.2.2. Geographic Scope of the Environmental Problem

The most important characteristic, however, to distinguish whether trade measures are legitimate or not, concerns the geographic scope of the environmental problem in question. The argumentation is different when the environmental problem is global in nature (with the most prominent examples being the greenhouse effect or ozone depletion), or, while not fully global, has impacts that cross borders (transboundary problems, e.g. sulfur dioxide emissions in Europe), versus problems when the environmental conduct has "only" national or local effects. Even though in a world with complex ecological interlinkages many actual problems can admittedly not fully be captured within only one category, this distinction is helpful for setting forth the issue.

---

44 GATT Secretariat (1992), p. 38.
45 Zarsky (1991), p. 64.
46 Compare section II.3.1.
47 Proposal put forward for example by Zarsky (1991), p. 70.

2.2.2.1. Global and Transboundary Environmental Problems

Again it is evident that the first best solution is a global *environmental* agreement. For cases where this cannot be achieved countries usually will be considered to have a larger stake in trade measures as they are also environmentally affected by foreign countries´ environmental activities. For each country any contribution to safeguarding the global commons has a public good element. Countries that seek to contribute to the global commons more than other countries may want to resort to trade measures in order to:

(a) convince other countries to join an international environmental agreement or to behave according to certain environmental norms; such that they
(b) prevent other country's actions from undermining their own environmental efforts; and
(c) deny other countries economic gains from failing to follow such norms; which is the same as preventing their own environmentally regulated industries from experiencing competitive disadvantage in the home market.

Such trade measures can either be considered in the form of direct trade interventions which impact directly on the perceived problem (such as trade bans or countervailing levies for lower regulated foreign industries) or in the form of rather indirectly functioning trade inducements, namely sanctions or incentives that are taken with respect to unrelated products (such as the US-Mexico NAFTA negotiations for open market access in return for reduced transborder pollution). The latter being a political instrument, we shall only investigate the economic effects of the former. The subsequent political reasoning in both cases is similar.

Any ban or border adjustment measure cannot give rise to the optimal solution anymore. First, it only effects a (small) part of production in the low-regulating country, the part that is exported to the counterbalancing country. Second, a country's decision on the level of the border adjustment measure usually will not take into account any production externality effects that arise in a third or fourth country.[48] Nevertheless, without being optimal, it may be considered beneficial for one or more of the reasons stated above.

For transboundary pollution the case is equivalent. Again a full cooperative solution would be preferable, where each country considers in its level of environmental production regulation all externalities caused by its production, regardless of where they accrue, inside or outside its borders. Trade measures might again be considered, this time only for the subset of countries involved in transborder pollution creation or receival, with the additional difficulty of distinguishing between countries according to the different impact pollution generated within them causes.

There is currently rather broad consensus that trade measures should be a legitimate instrument for this category of global and transboundary pollution, if they are, most importantly, part of a *multilateral agreement*. Most authors also indicate that first other forms of non-trade inducements have to be similarly considered, such as technical or financial aid, and when nevertheless trade measures are taken, they also should as much as possible take the form of trade inducements (positive incentives). Such proponents include Subramanian (1992) and Pearson and Repetto (1991).

There are other voices who also consider such trade measures legitimate when taken unilaterally, as these authors consider international agreements potentially may take too long to be agreed upon or not stringent enough. For example, Shrybman´s (1989) proposal for a GATT Article XX amendment to allow for any action necessary to protect the environment, including the establishment of import or export restrictions, or the use of subsidies, can be regarded in this line.

The work of the OECD working group currently underway can be expected to represent the first broad official consensus on this issue.

---

[48] Baumol and Oates (1988) is one of the few environmental textbooks considering the trade and environment interlinkage; chapter 16.

2.2.2.2. National and Local Environmental Problems

For this category of environmental problems the discussion is much more controversial. Members of the trade community usually strongly deny the appropriateness of trade measures for the solution of national environmental problems, the difference in environmental endowments and preferences being one of the very reasons for the benefits of international trade. Siebert (1992) for example states, that

> environmental abundance or scarcity is a factor in foreign trade which should be included in determining comparative advantage like other traditionally recognized factors, such as resources, technical know-how, and so on. It would not make sense that pressure groups with strong interests (export and import industries, unions) attempt to compensate for the environmental advantages of other countries through trade-policy measures. By levying tariffs on imports or subsidizing their exports, environmentally poor countries might attempt to protect their domestic industries that produce pollution-intensive goods. For economic reasons they might try to counteract their own environmental-policy measures. The costs of such a policy are bound to be high in the long run since such a policy means that each country will try to compensate its comparative disadvantage by policy measures. A country poorly endowed with labor will protect itself against labor-intensive imports; a country poorly endowed with capital will protect itself against capital-intensive imports; ..... In such a scenario, the idea of the advantages of international specialization is dead.[49]

Two main lines of argumentation run contrary to this basic trade view. Some economists argue against it for political reasons. They do not see the danger of environmental conditionality later being demanded similarly to counter other intercountry differences. But they consider the environmental concern to be so strong, that when not adjusting current trade regulation, they fear for a continuously smoothly functioning international trade system. Uimonen and Whalley (1991), for example, suggest,

> [...] that despite the concern from trade policy circles that exceptions from trade disciplines on environmental grounds create precedents for other non-

[49] Siebert (1992), pp. 173-174.

> trade uses of trade policy (workers rights, human rights), the strength of public concern over environmental issues seems likely to force some form of accomodation of trade rules to environmental concerns. .. This could take the form of general environmental exceptions to trade rules, new waiver arrangements, or piecemeal rule by rule rewriting. Longer term, we suggest that new global institutional approaches could be called for.[50]

The other line of argument is put forward by parts of the environmental community. Basically, it rests on attaching more importance to increased environmental burden due to trade than to any other gains that arise from trade. In the diagramatic analysis of section 2.1.2., proponents of this group would view the governmental optimal environmental policy to be such that any additional pollution due to the opening to trade is prevented, and if this is politically not achievable, that trade restrictions would have to be implemented for this purpose.

A second argument concerns the definition of "national or local environmental problems". In the real world environmental effects often can hardly be restricted to small geographic areas, and drawing any line between local and non-local effects is necessarily arbitrary. For example,

> [...] locally used toxic substances can be transported far from their points of origin. E.g., pesticides, polychlorinated biphenyls (PCBs), lead, and dioxines are found in Arctic regions, including potentially hazardous levels of PCBs in the breast milk and blood of Inuit people in northern Quebec.[51]

Therefore, in our world of complex ecological links, it is concluded, environmental effects are hardly ever purely national or local, such that the global community almost always has at least some stake in them. Considering them only local may be a fallacy that might be regretted later.

A third argument is put forward by the concept of the "ecological footprint" of regions, brought into discussion by Wackernagel and Rees (1992a). They calculated the land area required implicitely to support and

---

[50] Uimonen and Whalley (1991), abstract; see also pp. 58-60.
[51] U.S. Congress (1992), p. 47.

maintain current consumption levels of typical industrial regions and found that these regions usually appropriate the bioproduction of about 10 to 20 times more land than is contained within their actual borders. This, in general, might not be viewed problematic. For environmental problems, however, it can be argued that they are much better solved, when they are directly recognized by the population as such. Local environmental problems therefore have been addressed in the past much more effectively than global environmental problems. With nations depending in their consumption levels strongly on other often far away regions, and potentially causing environmental problems there, the link to direct observation of the problem by the user causing it, may be much harder to observe, and the environmental problem thus addressed much later or not at all.

Favoring trade interventions also for the case of national environmental problems obviously can immediately be challenged as containing some elements of "environmental colonialism", not granting the foreign country full sovereignty in choosing its preferred environmental quality level independently by introducing the relevant domestic environmental policy itself. It has to be added that this in fact is only true for the part of production the foreign country would export to the countervailing country. For domestic consumption the foreign country would still be free to strike its preferred balance of environmental quality and production of goods.

Effectively, the controversy on this issue is a political one. Turning to the philosophy of politics therefore promises to enhance our evaluation. A contribution by Sloterdijk in this field interprets current politics as potentially taking one of two possible forms, following "the fundamental" or "the urgent"[52]. In the historical perspective since absolutism, and more evidently since the French revolution, he sees politics as more and more putting decision structures (and approval by the people) above the burning throng of problems. In the current understanding, individuals can only become political subjects when they neglect their authentic existence as

[52] German original: Das Grundsätzliche und das Dringliche, Sloterdijk (1989), pp. 211 - 243; own translations.

defined by their passions, and reduce themselves to mere subjects of rational interests. As politics thereby excludes "the most important" it looks for ways to compensate this deficiency and can find it by representing "fundamentals", which grants identity with a broad base. In this way, politics gains credibility again. If consistently thought through to its end, it is, however, the arms system that essentially represents the embodiment of "fundamentals". As an alternative - especially in increasingly difficult problem situations - Sloterdijk sees politics as listening to the consciousness of the people, the politician as becoming the "medium of the urgent".

Our problem, in fact, is a representation of the struggle among and between these two possibilities. When we remain solely with interests, we can trust that each society will strike its own right balance between state of the environment and production, and consequently trade measures would be denied, given that the environmental problem is truly national. If, however, politics is seen as also having to listen to individual passions in the current complex problem situation, the case is open again. "The urgent" could turn out to also include trade interventions for only national or local environmental problems.

3. Opposing Demands for a Regulatory Change and its Paradigmatic Background

After the potential clash between trade and environmental policies was recognized, the last two to three years have seen an increasing number of proposals brought forward on how the international trade regulatory system would need to be changed (or, respectively, would not need to be changed), such that environmental concerns are well covered. Their conclusions cover a broad spectrum. When reviewing them, the differentiation of the problem along the criteria set forward above, is relevant for evaluating the (for the most part implicit) consequences of the regulation requested in each case, but cannot really explain the differences in opinion among the various proposals. If an explanation of these differences is sought - a most helpful ingredient to clarify the discussion - it appears to be much better found when the proposals are linked to the paradigmatic background of how the relationship between economy and environment is viewed - the task pursued in this section.

3.1. Paradigms of the Interrelationship between Economy and Environment

While there is no unambiguous general classification of views on the economy-environment interrelationship, a classification by Colby (1990) as set out in a World Bank Discussion Paper has received broad acceptance.

Earlier contributions describing the development of approaches for the environment-economy interface include Cleveland (1987), Martinez-Allier (1987), Turner (1988), Barbier (1989), Clark (1989) and Mirowski (1989). The main text book on environmental economics, Pearce and Turner (1990), summarizes in a historical perspective how the classical, Marxist, neoclassical and humanist, but also the institutional and coevolutionary paradigms have influenced the development of environmental economics. Folke and Kaberger (1991) exemplifies one study that especially points out the classification by Colby, as he,

> [...] has contributed to the understanding [that a pluralistic view of the contribution that economics can make would guard against narrowness in economics] by synthesizing many ideas and perspectives from the scientific literature and the environmental debate.

Colby proposes five broad paradigms of human-nature relationship, each based on different assumptions about human nature and activity, about nature itself, and about the interactions between nature and humans:

(1) Frontier economics: Common to both decentralized capitalist and centrally-planned Marxist economies, this paradigm dominated up until the late sixties. Nature is treated as being in both of its production-related aspects infinite, as a source of supply of physical resources and as a sink for the by-products. As natural resources are not considered scarce, nature

does not enter into the predominant economic thinking. The approach to nature is to concentrate on technologies and strategies that increase harvest rates (e.g. industrial agriculture). Damage that might arise is seen as in any case repairable due to technological change and economic growth.

(2) Deep ecology: Under this name Colby formulates a worldview that "has been widely interpreted as the polar opposite of frontier economics." It synthesizes philosophical, ethical, social and spiritual aspects that have been downplayed in the above paradigm.

> Deep ecologists promote merging an understanding and appreciation of some of the more technical, scientific aspects of systems ecology with a non-anthropocentric, "biocentric," or "harmonious" view of the relationship between man and nature, which often means putting man under nature, the reverse of the frontier economics hierarchy.

Central concerns are biospecies equality, bioregional autonomy, promotion of biological and cultural diversity, and decentralized planning utilizing multiple value systems. Technological fixes are seen in this paradigm as often creating larger, more costly and more intractable problems. The main criticism is that, while the ultimate imperative of an "anti-growth 'Eco-topia', of a constrained 'harmony with nature'" may be organic, it tends not to allow for sufficient creativity, which, however, is crucial for both nature and human society.

Out of these two diametrically opposed and dichotomous paradigms, perspectives are currently evolving that increasingly integrate economic, ecological and social systems aspects:

(3) Environmental protection: When environmental problems were recognized, the paradigm of "frontier economics" was modestly adjusted. The approach is defensive in practice, concerned mainly with ameliorating the effects of human activities. The focus is on damage control by institutionalising repairing and the setting of limits to harmful activities. The main criticism on this "end-of-the pipe" or "business-as-usual, plus a treatment plan" approach is that remedial measures are usually much more expensive than prevention. For the latter, a much better understanding of

nature and its actual interdependence with the economy would be necessary.

(4) Resource management: In direct contradiction to frontier economics, in this paradigm, the exhaustion of natural resources in this paradigm becomes a main concern. Recognizing that our societies, especially developing economies, depend on a much broader definition of nature, the request is to incorporate all kinds of capital (biophysical, human, infrastructural, and monetary) into calculations of national accounts, productivity, and economic policy and investment planning. This approach is the basic theme of reports such as the Brundtland Commission's *Our Common Future*, and the World Resources Institute's (bi)annual *World Resources* reports. The neoclassical imperative of economic growth appears to be still the primary goal, but sustainability is viewed as a necessary constraint for 'green growth'. The main objective in order to reach 'global efficiency' is to correct the incentive system for the individuals, such that economic market forces ensure efficient environmental management (e.g. by the introduction of tradeable permits schemes).

(5) Ecodevelopment: This is seen as the paradigm potentially for the longer term future that arises out of the shortcomings of environmental protection and resource management.

> It more explicitely sets out to restructure the relationship between society and nature into a 'positive sum game' by reorganizing human activities so as to be synergetic with ecosystem processes and services. [...] It would attempt to move from polluter pays to "pollution prevention pays".

It seeks to decouple economic growth from growth in the biophysical level. Ultimately there are of course limits to that,

> [...] but there is also room for great improvement, not just in efficiency as it is conventionally thought of, but in terms of synergies gained from designing agricultural and industrial processes to mimic (and to use) ecosystem processes (e.g., in turning the unused byproducts of one production process into the inputs for another[53]).

[53] For this example see in full detail Schwarz (1994).

The younger literature often labels this approach "co-evolutionary development" between man and nature.[54] The basic question would move from "How can we create and then how can we remedy?" towards "How can we create ecologically?".

3.2. Conclusions for the Trade and Environment Relationship

Depending on the paradigmatic background, different aspects of the trade and environment interlinkage are emphasized more strongly, leading to different conclusions on the degree to which free trade can be supportive to environmental improvement, and thereby determining the degree to which trade measures for environmental purposes are approved.

3.2.1. Frontier Economics and Environmental Protection

Under the paradigm of 'frontier economics', as the environment is generally not seen to be a scarce resource, environmental policy is not evaluated to be an area to which priority must be given. Any conflict between trade and environment is seen as rather fictituous, because within the economic process, the means are generated to address new scarcities that might eventually evolve.

The interlinkage most emphasized is that of societies increasing in wealth also devoting more of their resources to environmental improvement. Recently, this aspect has been empirically analyzed - among other issues - in Grossman and Krueger (1991). When comparing sulfur dioxide and smoke levels in several cities with differing income levels, they found levels of these pollutants rising as per capita income rose until a level of US$ 5000; then, the pollutant levels declined as per capita income rose further, up until about US$ 15 000 per year, after which per capita emissions began to rise again. This most likely is due to increasing demand for environmental quality which is translated into environmental protection laws and enforcement. More prosperous societies in general also prefer less pollution-intensive industries. Insofar as trade promotes

[54] See Norgaard (1988).

growth, it is a necessary ingredient to benefit the environment via this link. Critics remark that, nevertheless, at least currently, those countries with the highest per capita income levels also are the largest contributors to many environmental problems. "The United States, for example, contains 5 percent of the world's population, but accounts for 20 percent of global warming potential and 20 to 30 percent of emissions of major ozone-degrading compounds CFC-11 and -12".[55]

Under the paradigm 'environmental protection' these scarcities are acknowledged, and solutions are sought by addressing them, mainly by the development of cleaner technologies. In addition to trade contributing to necessary growth, it's role in contributing to a better and faster international diffusion of environmentally preferable production technologies is emphasized. Birdsall and Wheeler (1991) provide some limited empirical evidence for this link, suggesting that in Latin American, relatively open economies are more likely to adopt cleaner technologies than are more closed economies. That this link, most importantly, is relevant for weak-standard countries is pointed out by U.S. Congress (1992):

> Such a result [of the Birdsall and Wheeler study, K.S.] may be due to the need of export-oriented industries in developing countries to meet more stringent product standards and customer demand in developed country markets (e.g., dioxine-free paper). Open economies may be more receptive to imports of foreign technologies that are cleaner and more efficient than older production processes. In some cases, multinational firms might bring technologies that meet corporate or home country standards which are more stringent than local requirements.[56]

One institution arguing under this paradigm, for example, is the U.S. Council for International Business:

> Economic growth provides the conditions in which protection of the environment can best be achieved and environmental protection, in balance with other goals, is necessary to achieve growth that is sustainable. [...] Open trade not only contributes to sustainable development by increasing economic

[55] U.S. Congress (1992), p. 39.
[56] ibid., p. 39.

> growth but also facilitates the adoption of needed environmental protection by providing access to goods and technologies that are environmentally advanced, and by minimizing waste through trade in recovered material for recycling.[57]

Consequently, for the regulatory reform, a strengthening of the free trade aspect is called for:

> Despite the lack of explicit reference to environmental protection in GATT Article XX on exceptions, the language of this article is so broad that it is difficult to challenge exceptions taken for environmental purposes. In fact, domestic environmental regulations have rarely been challenged, but we believe present GATT rules are not strong enough to prevent abuse of national environmental regulations for trade protection purposes.[58]

Specific recommendations then include, for example, "Government subsidies to enterprises for environmental purposes, which are sectorally or regionally specific, and which cause injury to other parties, should remain actionable under GATT rules."[59]

3.2.2. Resource Management

Proposals mainly devoted to this paradigm put more emphasis on potential environmental shortcomings of trade, and for these cases claim priority for environmental concerns.

First, this concerns trade in products that are not well managed domestically, and results in proposals of trade restrictions for wild species or timber contingent on domestic sustainable resource management. In this line Burgess (1991) for wild species and Zarsky (1991) for tropical timber have been quoted earlier. Arden-Clark (1991) for that purpose specifically suggests for GATT that, "the exemption already incorporated in Article XX(g) should be ammended to read: 'measures relating to the conservation of exhaustible natural resources if such measures constitute an integral part of a sustainable management plan.'"[60]

---

[57] U.S. Council recommendations to the U.S. Government in May 1992, as cited in Gavin (1992).

[58] ibid. p. 79.

[59] ibid. p. 80.

[60] Arden-Clarke (1991), p. 6.

Second, proposals can be subsumed under this paradigm that seek a regulatory change to provide stronger incentives for national environmental policy, mainly by providing for border adjustment measures for environmental reasons (environmental conditionality). As international competition is one of the main obstacles in the implementation of new national environmental policy, it is argued that countries should be given at least the possibility of preventing foreign low-regulated products of competing in their home markets with their price wedge, by means of charging a correspondingly high border levy. Especially since countries that decide to introduce stricter environmental policy lose in export markets anyway. Some proposals also require the allowance for export subsidies on environmental regulation cost grounds.

Arden-Clark (1991) considers for this objective that the

> [...] simplest, and possibly most effective, way [...] is to amend [GATT] Article VI [anti-dumping-article, K.S.] in such a way as to recognize 'externalized' environmental and resource costs as an inadmissible subsidy. [...] In effect, the GATT would then establish full internalization of these costs as the international objective. Once this standard is met it should ensure that trade liberalization can be pursued in the certainty that it would contribute to environmental protection, efficient use of natural resources and sustainable development.[61]

This representing rather the long-term objective, for the interim period the proposal is that

> [environmental] exemptions should be extended to Article III to enable countries to 'protect' those domestic industries which have already internalized these costs and a relaxation of tariff binding regulations to allow for such adjustments; and Article XVI to allow for provision of export subsidies on the same basis. These exemptions could be created by strengthening Article XX.[62]

The main issue of discussion here, besides the fundamental question of legitimacy, is the administrative setup.[63]

---

61 ibid.

62 ibid.

63 See Steininger (1994) for the merits and shortcomings of two potential schemes for that end, based on product lifecycle analysis and cost share of environmental

3.2.3. Eco-Development

Thinking along the lines of eco-development emphasises most supply as being as local as possible and therefore trade is decreasing in importance for more products and natural resources. Trade, however, increases in importance in as far as the commodity is information.

The concept of the 'ecological footprint' or 'appropriated carrying capacity' of regions can be regarded as belonging to this paradigm. It initially points out the biophysical dependence of cities on their environs, later that of countries on other countries or continents.

> In ecological terms the city is a node of pure consumption existing parasitically on an extensive external resource base. While the latter may be spatially diffuse 'the relevant knowledge is that it must be somewhere, it must be adequate, it must be available, and it must grow if the city grows'.[64]

No such region, or similarly country, exists as an independent unit, but rather, they depend on trade for their survival. "Such regions are running an unaccounted ecological deficit - their populations are appropriating carrying capacity from elsewhere." Which, in itself, does not cause problems, as it also does not in ecological systems:

> Regional ecological deficits do not necessarily pose a problem if import-dependent regions are drawing on true ecological surpluses in the exporting regions. A group of trading regions remains within net carrying capacity as long as total consumption does not exceed aggregate sustainable production. The problem is that prevailing economic logic and trade agreements ignore carrying capacity and sustainability considerations. In these circumstances, [...] trade may actually accelerate the depletion of essential natural capital thereby undermining global carrying capacity.[65]

In their conclusions for international trade regulation, proposals derived therefrom meet with the demand for a "sustainable resource management

---

regulation, respectively. While the former is advisible for eco-labeling purposes, the latter turns out to be applicable on a much broader basis.

64 Wackernagel and Rees (1992b), p. 11, with a citation of R. Overby, 1985, The Urban Economic Challenge: Improvement of Human Welfare by Building and Managing Urban Ecosystems, mimeo, Washington, D.C.: The World Bank.

65 ibid. p. 8.

certificate"-contingency of free trade in natural resources as mentioned above. As such regulation, however, depends on every country actually implementing corresponding measures, this would be seen as potentially not sufficient, as quite a bit of the essential natural capital might nevertheless be overexploited. To prevent such a development, it is suggested that the trade agreement itself be formalized in terms of carrying capacity (Rees 1992), such that "a shift from the present emphasis on global economic integration and inter-regional dependency toward greater regional autonomy and self-reliance"[66] can be achieved.

3.3. Conclusion for Further Regulatory Development

With the most relevant international working groups on the trade and environment issue still trying hard to find consensus, it appears to be too early to reach conclusions for any particular changes in the trade regulation framework besides those laid down in the Uruguay Round Final Act. But from the analysis in this chapter more general conclusions can be drawn.

Differences in opinion being that broad, and especially since they are based rather on differences in the paradigmatic background, they will hardly be easily overcome such that consensus is reached with the acceptance of only one line of thought.

In what direction is country latitude in environmental regulation likely to develop? With respect to the currently wide range of country independence in environmental *product* regulation it is foreseeable that there will be further successful agreements on narrowing this independence by international harmonization of standards and standard testing procedures, thus reducing trade barriers and intercountry conflicts.[67] Yet, some scope for independent and unilateral national regulation definitely will remain as countries natural endowments and preferences differ.

---

66 ibid. p. 15.

67 An exemplifying step in this direction has been recently set by the Sanitary/ Phytosanitary Agreement within the Uruguay Round Final Agreement.

With respect to environmental process regulation the likely tendency of development is in the opposite direction, giving more weight to environmental over trade concerns. Current GATT regulation grants counterbalancing measures only for one case, namely that of imposing equivalent import charges on like products that carry domestic environmental taxes, if this tax is levied directly on the product. While this will be sustained also in future regulation, there is quite some scope that the countervailability might be extended to more cases of regulation. The likelihood is even higher for its alternative, namely that of allowing for at least some categories of environmental subsidies. Within the Uruguay Round Final Act the latter has already come true with respect to subsidies up to 20% of the cost of new equipment due to environmental regulation on a one-time basis.[68] But it is very unlikely, that in the future considerations will be extended that far that countervailability is permitted for the full (investment and operating) cost caused by all national environmental regulation. This is definitely seen as either administratively not to be handled and/or therefore imposing too much of a protectionist risk on the international trade system.

Nations will therefore also in the future have the option of independently choosing stricter environmental process regulation policy in areas for which regulation costs are not countervailable at the border. In other words, for quite a range of potential environmental regulation, countries pursuing these will incur an (at least short term) competitive disadvantage.

The question of weighing these short term economic effects, potential long term economic effects, and environmental effects of national environmental policy, therefore will be a very crucial one in a country's effort to employ policies towards sustainability. It therefore is the topic of chapter IV.

For a European country approaching EU membership it may be argued that EU harmonization of environmental policy will strongly diminish this effect. As was pointed out in section III.1.3., however, EU law allows for

---

68 See section III.1.1.1. for the further requirements of subsidies to be actionable.

unilateral stricter environmental process regulation, and it is to be assumed that with increasing environmental problems countries will have to take this option more and more to solve problems before the community can agree on common regulation. Additionally, even when there is common regulation, as was pointed out specifically, there is often very slow implementation or none at all in quite some countries, which effectively puts the complying countries into the same "unilateral" position, though unintentionally. The question analyzed below therefore arises equivalently for countries within or outside EU regulation.

IV

DIVERGENT ENVIRONMENTAL PROCESS REGULATION IN OPEN ECONOMIES

1. Theoretical Approaches

Two classes of economic relations have to be distinguished:

- For environmental regulation affecting trade in goods categories that are homogenous, the main causation will run along the line of comparative advantage. For the analysis of these goods flows, therefore, traditional trade theory shall be employed. In geographic terms the issue for industrialized countries' environmental regulation here is that of a competitive threat mainly by economically rather different countries, e.g., for Austria by Eastern European as well as Third World Countries.

- A much larger fraction of trade, however, takes place in the form of cross-hauling within the same sector among very similar countries. Here it is product differentiation that explains trade flows. For this category of trade flows it is new trade theory that gives us the best instrumentarium at hand, as it incorporates product differentiation and its consequences, increasing returns to scale and imperfect competition.

Models of economic geography can be applied to both classes, whereas the field at the intersection of new growth and new trade theory, the theory of innovation, will rather help to understand effects within the second class, in particular dynamic developments in trade among developed economies.

1.1. Effects of Environmental Policy in a Traditional Trade Theory Model

The most straightforward procedure to include environmental policy in traditional trade models is to show its effect on the production possibility frontier of a country.[1] This can be done in a model of production for two consumer goods that are produced by a single factor of production Q (which can represent a vector of factors), and emissions S which are produced as joint products in this process. There are various fixed processes of joint production, such that the overall technology is one of variable joint production. Technical progress is excluded for the moment.

The factor of production, Q, cannot only be used to produce the commodities, but also to clean up emissions. The remaining emissions (net emissions) are deposited into the environment. They can be viewed as a factor of production, as the assimilative capacity of the environment.

For each consumer good a functional relationship between produced quantity and used amounts of factors Q and S ("assimilative capacity") can be given:

$x_i = F_i(Q_i, S_i)$, the net-emission production function.

Q measures the factor-input in both production and clean up.

Good 1 is assumed to be the emission-intensive one, i.e. $S_1/Q_1 > S_2/Q_2$.

Under the additional assumption of declining partial marginal productivities for Q and S the space of transformation has the shape given in Figure 4.1.

[1] The exposition in this section 1.1. as well as the respective figures 4.1 to 4.3 closely follow Wießner (1991), chapter 3.

Figure 4.1: Production Possibility Space Considering Environmental Quality

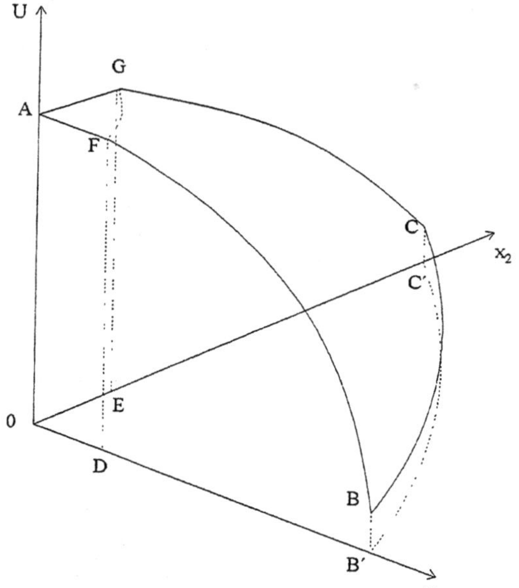

Source: Siebert (1992), p. 33

If the factor Q is used fully for goods production, an amount of B' of good 1 or C' of good 2 can be produced. The resulting environmental quality is lower in the case of the emission-intensive good 1. C'B' is the traditional production possibilty frontier, when there is no clean-up activity.

OA is the maximal possible environmental quality, when there is no production at all. As Q can be used for emission clean up, it is possible to have production while keeping this environmental quality. Production beyond GF is only possible when Q is no longer used for cleaning up all emissions. From OD to OB' emissions increase more than output as marginal productivity declines in both production and clean up. FB has a concave shape.

The biological assimilative capacity and the societal choice of the desired environmental quality determine together the environmental index level that is aimed at. The horizontal cut of the transformation space at this level determines the now relevant production possibility frontier (PPF).

When even by sole production of the emission-intensive good the environmental quality is still above this level, the PPF is unchanged. When the restriction becomes binding only in the case towards full production of x_1, but not towards the sole production of x_2, the PPF is changed to AB_1 in Figure 4.2. If the chosen level represents a restriction for any production, irrelevant of its mix, a PPF of A_1B_1 follows.

Figure 4.2: Production Possibility Frontier at Different Levels of Environmental Standard

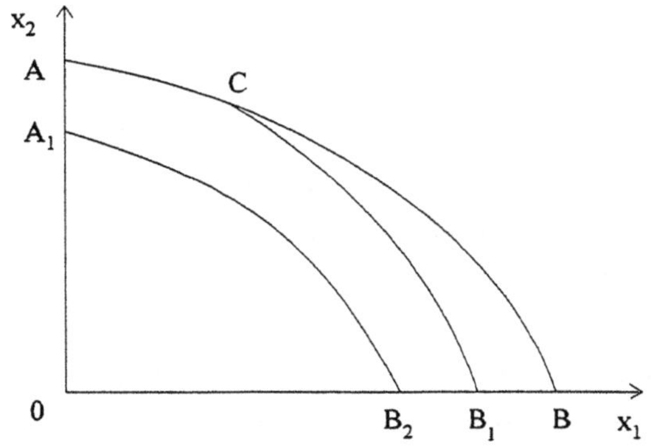

Source: Gronych (1980), p. 141

The effects of unilateral environmental policy now can be determined by the effects on the relative prices that a leftward shift of the PPF causes. Assuming the general case that in the original situation national prices differ across countries (i.e. different PPFs) gives the PPF AB in Figure 4.3. for the home country and CC for the foreign country. This also assumes that the home country has a comparative advantage in the emission-intensive good 1 in the original situation.

When the home country introduces stricter environmental policy the net effect on the resulting trade flows remains ambiguous. Depending on its

Figure 4.3: Comparative Cost Advantage for the Home Country Pursuing Environmental Policy

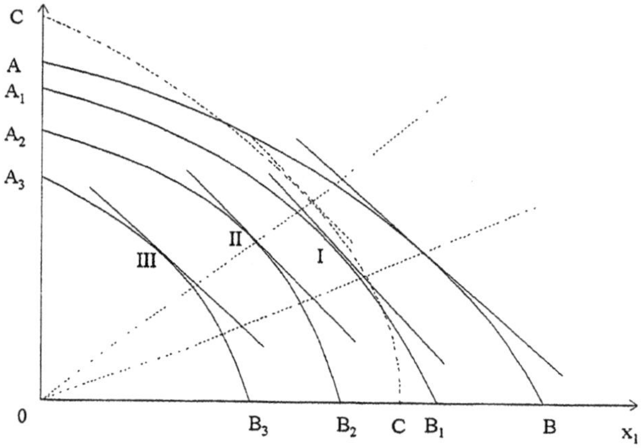

Source: Wießner (1991), p. 90

stringency, the original comparative advantage remains (I), is exactly counterbalanced in the border line case (II), or is turned around (III). Specialization of the home country is reduced in quantities in any case, but not necessarily turned around.

The general conclusion from traditional trade models is always that the country that introduces stricter environmental policy experiences increased specialization in the production of the low-emission good. The reason being a relative cost increase in the production of the other, high-emission good.

1.2. Economic Geography and the Choice of Clean Industry Location

For environmental policy analysis dynamic considerations are of particular importance, not only for the environmental benefits involved, but also for the long-term effects on the production and trade structure.

To that end the theory of economic geography takes up the discussion of scale effects again, that Alfred Marshall already emphasized, though now more formalized: the advantages of labor-pooling, proximity of intermediate input suppliers and technological spillovers. It no longer views countries as dimensionless points that carry out trade, but reintroduces the concept of space into economic theory.[2]

For the purpose of this study the one type of reasoning most clearly observable in production statistics can be focused on: intermediate input flows. A simple and supportive analysis of enterprise location decision can be carried out by relating fixed costs and transport costs involved in this decision process.

Let us assume an enterprise in the new clean-up sector has to decide in which country it will produce. Further, we assume that the final demand should be 60% of the sector's output, whereas the remaining 40% is intermediate input demand by the sector itself. The firms' costs are given in table 4.1 (see next page) for the case that total output be 10 units, fixed costs be 4 units and transport costs per unit produced be 4. As the decision of each firm is dependent on the location decision of all other firms in this sector, we get a multiple equilibrium at the assumed cost structure. Output in this new sector is either produced in both countries or in one of the two.[3] Once a production location structure is established it remains self-enforcing.

If a country now starts to produce in a sector earlier than others, it can cause that country to remain the long-term single world producer of these commodities. Insofar as environmental policy causes the creation of sectors embodying such a cost structure, early and strict environmental policy has a positive foreign trade effect.

A second reasoning is implicit in the model. Multiple equilibria exist when there are substantial fixed costs (and thereby increasing returns to scale), but only if they are not too large relative to the transport costs.

---

[2] Among the very few publications (outside strict regional economics) Krugman (1991) supplies a very lucid introduction into a range of basic ideas.

[3] Krugman (1991) focuses on regional specialization within a country. In the model employed in this section his reasoning is expanded to inter-country specialisation, deviating from Krugman by the treatment of intermediate inputs as tradeables.

When environmental policy increases transport costs, in some sectors they will become too large relative to the fixed costs, and formerly highly concentrated production will be split up into various sites. Overall world trade volume will then be reduced. For some countries this may mean substantial new local production.

Tab. 4.1. Enterprise Location Decision

Assumptions:
Sectoral Output: 10 Units
Final Demand: 60%
Sectoral Demand: 40%
Fixed Cost: 4
Transport Cost per Unit: 10

Location of other enterprises of the sector		Cost of typical enterprise, if it locates in: A	both sites	PL
A	fix	4	8	4
	transport	3	0	7
	total	7	8	11
50:50	fix	4	8	4
	transport	5	0	5
	total	9	8	9
PL	fix	4	8	4
	transport	5	0	5
	total	11	8	7

But environmental policy also increases fixed costs. This effect is much stronger for existing production than for new machinery to be installed. For new production sites, as they are dicussed here, it is much more the expectations of future costs that influence the location decision. Here the enterprise will decide to locate in that country which pursues a calculable and future-oriented environmental policy. The initially somewhat higher investment costs due to stricter environmental policy are a lot smaller than subsequent adjustment to a later standard change in the other country.

These dynamic effects mentioned are important counterbalancing mechanisms to the standard argument of comparative disadvantage. They therefore play an important role in the explanation of the broad empirical phenomenon that environmental policy did not cause or at the most hardly caused negative growth and trade balance effects, which will be surveyed in section 2.

Yet, it is not only the location of *environmental* industries and transport costs affected by environmental policy in an imperfect competition setting. The next section will broaden the analysis.

1.3. Environmental Policy and Strategic International Trade

For many industries the assumption of competitive markets is quite appropriate and reasoning along the lines of comparative costs will give the relevant conclusions for environmental policy. For other industries, however, the production and market structure are much better characterized by imperfect competition. In these cases environmental policy will have additional and at the outset often unexpected effects on the firms' decisions on output, size of capital investment and location.

As imperfect competition generates rents, it can cause strategic behavior to "grab these rents". Strategic behavior can be pursued on one hand by producers, and then be affected by the environmental policy chosen by the government. On the other hand, governments themselves could seek to use environmental policy to substitute for other non-available trade instruments to manipulate trade. Analyzing the latter case will give insights into the reasons for particular stringency levels chosen that cannot be justified solely on environmental grounds.

1.3.1. Environmental Policy Affecting Strategic Producer Behavior

In a situation of imperfect competition producers may seek to obtain larger market shares by commitments to a chosen level of capital investment and/or the choice of their production location.

Recent initial analysis conclusions show that these decisons can be crucially affected by environmental policy, namely by both the instrument and the level chosen. Ulph A.(1993) compares the effects of environmental policy using price instruments (taxes) versus quantity instruments (standards). He concludes that the incentive for firms for strategic overinvestment in capital is much lower when pollution standards are implemented than when taxes are used. Overinvestment being inefficient, welfare can therefore be enhanced by the use of standards. According to Ulphs calculations with world data from the fertilizer industry, the welfare gains connected with the choice of the instrument are of the same order of magnitude as the welfare gain by the reduction in emissions itself.

The superiority of standards, however, only holds if all countries aim to reduce emissions. When only some countries act unilaterally, the use of standards would cause a much larger loss of market shares to free riders than the use of taxes does, making the latter preferable overall. Again the potential assumption that imperfect competition would rather shelter industries and reduce the magnitude of welfare effects in cases when countries choose divergent environmental policies does not hold. As Ulph A.(1993) shows, in a setting with imperfect competition environmental policy will have even stronger welfare effects as it not only changes the costs of production but also affects the strategic behavior of producers.

Even the direction of the price change in national markets that environmental policy causes can be reversed in situations characterized by imperfect competition. In a model with endogenous location Ulph A.(1992) shows that a high environmental tax level can cause increased competition between producers in this market, causing output prices to *fall* due to substantial pollution taxes. Much smaller taxes on the other hand can lead to a substantial increase in output prices as competition is reduced. The results are due to the fact that the basically three factors driving the location decision of producers (divergencies across countries in fixed costs, in environmental taxes and in the level of competitiveness prevailing in the markets) are dominated by the last factor when the model is calibrated to data of the world fertilizer industry, as Ulph does.

Due to the complexity of imperfect competition strategic behavior multi-stage game models, it is usually not possible to solve them analytically.

The results of all these initial studies therefore depend on particular parameter settings, and are in that sense not robust. What the studies succeed in showing, however, is that the effects of environmental policy in markets with imperfect competition can be much more complex than in competitive ones.

1.3.2. Environmental Policy as a Strategic Trade Instrument of Governments

As governments are prohibited by international trade agreements from using a specified range of trade instruments they may be tempted to substitute by using environmental policy to manipulate trade in imperfect competition settings.

Even though there truly is a scope for strategic policy in such cases, the form of the optimal intervention depends crucially on assumptions about the behavior of agents. Ulph A. (1991) shows that assuming competition in quantities (Cournot) the government will set weaker standards than environmentally optimal. If it chooses the tax instrument the outcome will be even further from the environmentally optimal level. But if competition is assumed to take place rather in prices (Bertrand) the result is observed in the opposite direction, namely that governments will end up setting standards that are too tough. Ulph therefore concludes that the government may do best to focus on efficient environmental action for its own matters, as using this as a strategic policy instrument may worsen the situation substantially as it can easily go the wrong direction. The main focus of his study, however, is another conclusion: that environmental policy coordination can improve the welfare of both countries even if there is no transboundary pollution. Coordination will prevent countries from mutual strategic behavior locking them into an inferior Prisoner's Dilemma Nash-equilibrium.

Markusen et al. (1991) rather find the determining factor for the direction the government policy will go is in the size of the environmental damage costs. They conclude that, if they are low, governments will set standards that are too lax to attract production, whereas if they are high, they will set standards that are too strict to deter polluting production "from their back yard".

For the present study the results of this section 1.3. point out an important area for caution. For exposed industries, where imperfect competition prevails at the world level, there can be substantial reason to exempt them from national environmental policy regulation beyond what the competitive models already suggest. Such exemption would avoid welfare losses by strategic government behavior in the wrong direction.

Secondly, the gains from cooperation in environmetal policy regulating these industries may therefore also be larger than suggested by competitive modeling.

1.4. Environmental Policy, Innovation and Competition

A further major dynamic impact environmental policy involves is the triggering of innovation. In this process, however, there again may be reasons for the government to get involved.

Carraro and Siniscalco (1992) analyze the case of innovation for the exposed sectors of the economy. Emission reducing innovation represents the alternative to the reduction of output levels in order to meet emission requirements. As innovation is costly (both in terms of fixed investment and R&D) they conclude for different market structures (perfect competition, Bertrand and Cournot oligopoly) that in all of them international competition demands the government to subsidize innovation.

In subsequent analysis in Carraro and Topa (1992) it is left to the firm to decide whether to react to environmental regulation by output reduction or adopting new, environmentally-friendly, technology. Given that innovation is costly, firms experience an incentive to delay innovation. Again, the government can improve welfare by subsidizing innovation, more importantly so when environmental policy is set unilaterally.

A different line of the analysis of innovation is supplied by Ulph D.(1992). He focuses on the effects of strategic behavior of firms in their decision whether to devote resources to R&D in order to discover new "environmentally friendly" technology. While capturing two different types of R&D competition (a non-tournament form of competition where firms are able to innovate simultanously, and a tournament form of competition where firms race to be the first to discover a new technology), the main results for both are similar. Ulph shows that the general presumption that governments in such a situation become eager to introduce stricter standards does not hold. An increase in the environmental regulation level (he considers taxes, yet leaving the case open for standards) basically does not ensure that the firm in that country will undertake more R&D. In comparing the cases of unilateral and cooperative environmental policy his results supply no general conclusions, which is why he proposes the "examination of more specific examples - perhaps using numerical simulation".

Theoretical analysis of environmental innovation is a particularly young area of research. The reported results the international literature supplies so far are initial ones with further substantial contributions to be expected.

Overall, the last sections have pointed out that (especially for markets characterized by imperfect competition) there are a multitude of economic effects triggered by environmental policy; effects that often work in opposing directions. The size and direction of the net effect then is particularly a matter of empirical quantification, which we will turn to next.

2. Empirical Evidence

2.1. Environmental Policy Affecting Production and Trade

The first and more general question of environmental process regulation affecting the overall production level has been investigated by a large number of empirical studies since the early seventies. For their results the findings of a recent OECD study can serve as a good representative example. OECD (1991), analyzing the effects of environmental (i.e. pollution abatement and control) expenditure on output at the macroeconomic level in selected member countries, pointed out both positive and negative impacts. Positive impacts stemmed from increased job creation and the stimulation of some forms of technical change, while negative impacts were apparently the result of increased costs. The actual conclusion of this study, however, was that:

> At the aggregate level, the indirect economic impacts, whether positive or negative, were very small and were indeed an insignificant factor in the overall performance

of the six countries studied.[4] It has to be noted that this result refers to the national level. At the regional or industry level economic impacts of environmental expenditure can still be relatively larger.

Our main interest is a more specific one, concerning the effects of environmental process regulation on *trade flows*. Studies in this area are scarcer than growth effect studies, but still there are quite a few. As those up to 1990 are comprehensively summarized in two articles[5], we will restrict ourselves - for matters of pointing out methodological differences - to only three studies in detail, including the recent Grossman and Krueger (1991) and Tobey (1991), and for comparison Robison (1988). Other more recent studies primarily concentrate on the relocation question and will be pointed out in the next section.

---

[4] OECD (1991), p. 256.

[5] Ugelow (1982) reviews the earlier studies done in the 70s; Dean (1992) surveys the studies done through 1990.

The broad overall finding of all of these studies can be summarized by stating that the effects of environmental regulation on trade patterns have been rather small, if present at all.

Dean's (1992) conclusions still carry over also to the studies completed after her survey article.

> The methodologies are quite varied, making comparisons between studies difficult. However, some generalizations can be drawn. First, estimates of total environmental control costs (ECC) by industry tend to be very low -- abatement costs are a very small portion of industry costs on average. Second, reductions in output caused by ECC are also small and insignificant on average, although they can be significant for some individual sectors. Third, there is little evidence of any significant impact of ECC on the pattern of trade.[6]

For the two steps of analysis, the determination of environmental control costs and the testing of their trade impact, there are two broad methodological approaches.[7] For environmental control costs, one can either rely on statistical (time series) data available, or deduce the costs (namely direct and indirect) on the basis of an input-ouput model of the economy. Consequently, in the second step the statistical data is used in a regression framework to determine the significance of its trade impact, whereas the input-output model directly allows the quantification of the export and import impacts of a variation in ECCs.

The advantage of the statistical regression analysis is seen in the possibility of an examination on a very disaggregated industry level. The very strong limitation, obviously, is data availability. While data is ready for production and trade flows, environmental expenditure data access is very limited, especially if disaggregated data is sought. Also, data often is restricted to *direct* environmental control costs. The last point is the main reason for the application of input-output analysis that ensures that all cost components of environmental control, direct and indirect (price increases of intermediate inputs), are included. The limitation here is rather the - with increasing disaggregation - strongly growing demand for the construction of the input-output table.

---

[6] Dean (1992), p. 16.

[7] The classification has been explicitly introduced by Tudini (1993).

2.1.1. Recent Empirical Studies

Tobey (1991) constitutes the most comprehensive and recent regression analysis. He calculates total ECC as a percentage of total costs of production for 64 U.S. agricultural and manufacturing industries, and identifies 24 of them as pollution intensive, namely those exceeding an ECC share of 1.85%. He chooses a regression approach in the form of a (cross-section) Heckscher-Ohlin-Vanek model. He aggregates the pollution intensive industries into five groups and first analyzes the regression of U.S. net exports on U.S. endowments of 11 resources (capital, and various categories of labor, land and natural resources). The test is to introduce a dummy variable for environmental stringency as an additional explanatory variable, stating differences of policy and endowment in 23 countries, including developed, newly industrializing and developing countries. Tobey, in this test, was not able to find any significant influence of environmental regulation stringency on determining trade flows.[8]

Second, he employed an omitted variable test. If ECC do have an impact on net exports, then the sign of the error term should be different for countries with stringent versus lenient environmental regulation. Again, Tobey could not reject the null hypothesis, that there is no difference in the error terms sign, thus reconfirming the above conclusion.

Grossman and Krueger (1991), focusing on U.S.-Mexico trade, also applied regression analysis as one part of their study. The dependent variables in the three tests performed are U.S. imports from Mexico as a fraction of (a) total U.S. shipments, (b) Mexican value added and (c) the "maquiladora" value added.[9] Among the independent variables, they use in regression analysis, are human capital share, physical capital share, and pollution abatement cost as a fraction of industry value added. In all three

[8] In fact for only one industry group, chemicals, did the significance of the coefficient approach a conventionally accepted level of confidence, but with a sign of the coefficient indicating the reverse relationship, environmental regulation increasing export flows. A potential explanation could be a reputation effect in the chemicals industry sector.

[9] The maquiladora production comprises Mexican production in a tariff-exempted area bordering the U.S. (special Border Industrialization Program), especially accused of attracting U.S. industry by low regulation.

cases, they find the coefficient of pollution abatement control for the year 1987 to be not statistically significant.

Robison (1988) is the most comprehensive and recent study using an input-output approach. He again studies U.S. trade (for the years 1973, 1977, and 1982) with a twofold interest. First he calculates the pollution abatement content of U.S. trade. As ECC are hardly available for any trading partner, for evaluating U.S. imports, Robison, like practically all other existing studies in this field, has to use U.S. ECC of import-competing industries as a proxy for actual ECC of imports. His results indicate that the ratio of abatement content of U.S. imports to U.S. exports rose between 1973 and 1982 (from 1.151 to 1.389). He therefore concludes that U.S. comparative advantage has shifted away from goods which in the U.S. have high abatement costs. This shift is not experienced when only U.S. trade with Canada is looked at, pointing out that U.S. environmental regulation is closer to that of Canada than to that of all other trading partners considered together.

Second, he constructs a hypothetical scenario of an increase in abatement costs that raises the sectoral price level by 1%. For 78 sectors he calculates the impact on the 1977 sectoral trade balance of this scenario. The impacts he gets range from -0.12% (special industry machinery) to -7.08% (copper), with an average impact of -2.69%. For the aggregate trade balance the reduction in the value of total U.S. trade amounts to -0.67% for the 1977 input-output table. He thus finds that marginal changes in abatement costs will affect the U.S. balance of trade, though his figures suggest that this impact would be quite small on an overall level.

2.1.2. Limitations of the Studies

2.1.2.1. Determination of Environmental Control Costs

For both approaches, but especially so for the larger (time series) data demand for regression analysis, data availability of ECC is among the most severe limitations. Detailed time series on a disaggregated industry level hardly exist for any other country than the U.S.[10] But even where consistent data exists, its appropriateness is subject to discussion.

So, Tobey (1991) has been criticized by U.S. Congress (1992) for underreporting ECC in his study. Tobey - as most of the U.S. studies - uses pollution abatement expenditure from a survey by the Bureau of the Census. U.S. Congress states, that,

> [...] there is some evidence that these surveys underreport environmental control costs. For example, in the copper industry, Census data indicate that environmental control costs added 4 cents per pound to the price of copper in 1985. However, at least four other sources, based on actual examination of copper smelting firms, found that the expenses were much higher, ranging from 7.5 cents per pound to 15 cents per pound. The Census surveys may underreport true costs if the respondents do not have complete knowledge of all expenditures. Chapman [1991] found that survey results of the copper mining and smelting industry may not have included costs such as monitoring and planning activities, environmental activities that are part of the production process, interest expenses on equipment, and productivity loss.[11]

A second issue, beyond the quality of the data source, is to what data the ECC are related. As Kalt (1988) pointed out, there are two different ways to express environmental control costs. The first uses the share of environmental control costs paid directly by the firm as a ratio of value added. A second measure relies on the above mentioned input-output methodology and includes both the direct costs to the firm plus the indirect costs of environmental controls embedded in the firm's inputs and supplies. These costs are higher but they are divided by the total firm costs, not the lower value added. Some studies use direct environmental control costs as a share of total costs, rather than value added, which results in estimates that understate the true cost of environmental regulation.

---

[10] OECD (1991) is the broadest effort to collect pertinent data, though definition sometimes varies across countries. It supplies (i) pollution abatement control investments for public and private sector and (ii) pollution abatement expenditures; i.e. the sum of investment and current expenditure; for intercountry comparison both expressed as a percentage of GDP and (iii) index values of pollution control investment disaggregated by industry.

[11] U.S. Congress (1992), p. 101, fully referencing the four studies.

Tobey (1991) can be criticized on these grounds as well, as he relates direct environmental expenses to total costs. For the heavy polluting industries he gets a range of from 1.92 to 2.89%. A recent German study on the industry location effects of environmental regulation (Umweltbundesamt, 1993) gets industry ECC in the same - very low - percentage range. The reason is, that it also relates environmental expenses per industry sector (current costs and depreciation of environmental control equipment) to production value (equal to total costs), but not to the appropriate lower value added. For the manufacturing industries this study gets a range of from 0 (construction) to 2.6% (energy and mining), with an average of only 0.7%. However, Umweltbundesamt (1993) does not use these figures for any further trade regression analysis, but rather for inter-sector and inter-country location comparisons, such that the criticism is neutralized to a large part - but only for the particular question analyzed.

2.1.2.2. Time Period

All empirical studies focused mainly on the experience of the 60s and 70s, at the latest on the early eighties. Numerous authors point out that the importance of environmental costs is likely to increase in the future.

Tudini (1993) summarizes that "an update of the data that took into account the cost increase in the past decade and the foreseeable upward trend might lead to different findings."[12]

For the United States U.S. Congress (1992) states more specifically:

> It is important to note that much of the research dates to the 70s, and thus many of the conclusions [...] come from a time when U.S. industry was just beginning to feel the competitive pressures that have so greatly intensified in recent years. [...] Thus, while the studies generally concluded that the effects were small, this does not mean that these effects are currently insignificant and should not be addressed. [...] In an era of hightened competition, increased environmental costs can diminish trade performance, and when combined with

[12] Tudini (1993), p. 29.

> other effects (e.g., cost of capital, foreign industrial policies, etc.) may contribute to significant competitiveness difficulties.[13]

Also Tobey (1991) himself points out that "there is some evidence that there are fewer opportunities for inexpensive increments in the level of environmental quality than there have been in the past."[14] He cites Oates et al. (1989) estimating marginal abatement cost curves for controlling a common air pollutant in Baltimore. The study finds the (theoretically often assumed) fact that marginal abatement cost curves are fairly flat over a low range of environmental quality levels, but eventually begin to rise steeply as emissions are increasingly reduced. Moreover Oates et al. find that the intersection of current marginal benefits and marginal costs of pollution abatement is located at the base of the steep portion of the marginal cost curve. Increases in the demand for environmental quality therefore would entail large increases in the control costs. Whether this can be completely counterbalanced by technological change, alternative production techniques, or input substitutions remains questionable, as Tobey concludes.

While it appears very likely that ECC will increase, the actual amount of this increase also depends on the speed of the stepping up of stringency. In the Oates et al. framework it can be argued that once an environmental regulation is set, this gives the incentive for technological innovation, such that the flat (but nevertheless increasing) portion of the marginal cost of the abatement curve is extended, implying that the intersection with the marginal benefit curve (basically set by the public´s preferences) will - after the (potential) innovation - again rest at the base of the steep portion of the marginal abatement cost curve. Only when innovations or restructuring of the economy cannot be accomplished fast enough will the intersection move up more strongly, namely along the - in that case unshifted - steep portion of the marginal cost curve.

2.1.2.3. Benefits

None of the models include the benefits of environmental regulation - neither environmental improvements nor direct economic benefits - and as

[13] U.S. Congress (1992), p. 97.

[14] Tobey (1991), p. 16.

such may overstate the impact on trade. Direct economic benefits could result, first, from faster innovation. For example, U.S. Congress (1980) found that environmental regulation accelerated steel industry modernization. Pollution prevention efforts may also increase competitiveness when it, secondly, results in firms paying closer attention to energy and materials efficiency and continuous process improvement. The improvement of the environmental situation, thirdly, might be reflected in lower health care costs, higher agriculture and forestry output and lower costs in other parts of the economy from reduced pollution. Companies can benefit from these both directly and indirectly (cheaper supplies and inputs).

With respect to the dynamic effects, as was pointed out in the theoretical section IV.1.2, the country implementing environmental regulation first may receive some first-mover benefits. Finally, more stringent national environmental regulation will create advantages for the environmental protection industries, potentially increasing their (in stringent regulation countries traditional) sectoral trade surplus.

Summing up, the most severe limitations of empirical trade-impact-of-environmental-regulation studies have been the environmental control costs they are based upon, their time focus being in a past which is potentially not representative for the current situation, and the neglect of any of the benefits for the international economic position that environmental regulation also induces.

2.2. Environmental Policy Affecting Industry Location

For the focus on the second potential and even further reaching effect environmental policy can have, industry migration, discussion of the North American Free Trade Agreement, most especially, has triggered a number of empirical studies in our decade.[15] The standard comprehensive earlier reference is Leonard (1988).

---

[15] Many of them were completed for the Symposium on International Trade and the Environment, held at and sponsered by the World Bank in November 1991, published in Low (1992).

The U.S. Office of Technology Assessment gives a short summary of the results of these most recent, the Leonard and earlier studies:

> Studies of the location impact of environmental regulation are inconclusive, but suggest that the effect is modest. There are reasons to suggest that the migratory effect of environmental regulation is likely to be less than the trade effect. [...]
>
> For relocation decisions driven by cost considerations, the savings have to be large enough to overwhelm the cost of opening up a new plant (which can be substantial). Many firm location decisions are not driven by low cost, as access to markets, skilled labor, and quality infrastructure may be more important. And usually savings from lax environmental regulations will be relatively modest compared to the savings from other factors, such as low wages. However, many countries with low labor costs also have low levels of environmental and worker health and safety regulations, which when combined, can result in even lower costs.[16]

The reasoning within Europe with respect to this question is basically the same, as, for example, information supplied by the Austrian Business Council illustrates.[17]

In detail, Leonard (1988) presents case studies of U.S. foreign direct investment in Ireland, Spain, Mexico, and Romania. He argues that the industrial flight and pollution haven hypotheses are based on too static an idea of comparative advantage. Besides finding no evidence of large-scale industrial flight as a response to U.S. environmental regulation he sees "strong evidence" to suggest that deliberately attempting to attract foreign industry with low environmental regulation is "an extremely risky strategy". Companies attracted by such policies are likely to produce goods that are hazardous to use and manufacture. Exports run the risk of import barriers due to higher health and safety standards. Equally problematic is the likelihood that industries seeking a lax regulatory environment are declining or stagnant. While international flight might

[16] U.S. Congress (1992), pp. 99-100.

[17] Investigative talk with Erwin Bendl, Vereinigung Österreichischer Industrieller, Abteilung Industriepolitik, May 1993; see also Bendl (1993).

ensure short term survival, technological change will eventually make the industry uncompetitive.

Also, previous to Leonard, the earlier economy-wide statistical studies found no investment effect. The more recent ones sometimes do, but consider it insignificant.[18]

The results of surveys and case studies on the other hand show a somewhat mixed result.

For Germany, Umweltbundesamt (1993) concludes on the basis of company surveys that both for the early eighties and early nineties environmental expenses were not of significance in relocation decisions. It points out that in addition to the "hard" economic factors such as wage costs, productivity, and production relevant infrastructure, increasingly "soft" location factors gain importance, such as living and leisure value of regions, cultural and educational opportunities and image values. Such factors also are crucial in the recruitment of top level employees.

For the U.S. there are some surveys and case studies that suggest that lower environmental regulation does play a role. For example, Sanchez (1990) found that 26 percent of maquiladora operators in Mexicali cited Mexico's lax environmental enforcement as an important reason for their relocation (13 percent considered it a major factor, another 13 percent an important factor). Lesperance (1991), when studying the wood product coatings industry which is rather heavily regulated in California, finds employment shifts to Mexico.

Evidently case studies do find shifting effects, because some industries are more strongly affected by environmental regulation than others. In general, however, environmental compliance costs are likely to be an important factor only if the industry shows a special profile. In particular

[18] E.g., Low and Yeats (1992) cannot dismiss the fact that environmental standards have influenced firm location decisions, but regard it a rather insignificant part of the explanation for industry migration.
See Dean (1992) for a comprehensive survey of the earlier studies; Pearson and Repetto (1991) for one on the recent studies contained in Low (1992).

for the subset of industry that is (a) labor cost sensitive, (b) relatively footloose or is making new investment decisions, and (c) has high environmental compliance costs, low environmental regulation can add to the cost advantage gained by low labor cost.

The economy-wide overall migration effects due to environmental regulation that empirical studies found, have nevertheless been very modest so far, as this section pointed out.

3. Considerations for Austria

3.1. Environmental Control Costs

As the empirical studies have pointed out, ECC have been rather modest so far on an economy average level, but can reach significant levels for particular industry sectors. Looking for environmental expenditure data for Austria, there is only one source that disaggregates by industry sectors, Bundeskammer (1987, 1990, 1993). The Bundeskammer comprises company survey data it collected in 1974, 1978, 1983 and since in three-year intervals by questionaires distributed to its members of the section "industry". It is therefore rather "soft" data. The rate of returned questionaires has been relatively high, the data in this respect can be considered representative.[19] While the Bundeskammer sets the questionaire so that it can create a continuous yearly time series of environmental expenditures, the data of the years completed immediately before the respective investigations appears to be the most reliable as it draws on best remembrance within the companies. In fact, the tables show fluctuations in this respect and therefore most emphasis is put on multi-

[19] In terms of reacting companies the rate of return in all but the environmentally non-relevant film-industry has been between 60 and 80%. It dropped somewhat in the most recent 1992 survey. When it is considered that many small companies do not undertake environmental expenditures, but that rather the fewer larger ones do, who did respond, the representation is high. In terms of employees, respondence has been between 80 and 100%, in 1992 between 65 and 100%. Bundeskammer (1993), p. 8.

year averages. We shall rather concentrate on the pre-collection year data as it is likely to be closest to reality, thus the most recent are 1985, 1988 and 1991.

More limiting - especially for the international comparison - is another characteristic of the data. The survey collects total environmental expenditure undergone in one year (total environmental control equipment expenditure, operating expenses, and expenditure for compensations, for research and for recycling). It does not collect the data in a way that it can be related easily to the specific year of its use, i.e in an accounting "expense" sense. One would mainly need environmental equipment depreciation data rather than total expenditure data. As such, a calculation on the basis of the given data would have to rest on assumptions quite hypothetical; we shall rather remain with the data as aggregated by the Bundeskammer.[20]

To express ECC for interindustry and intercountry comparisons, either direct environmental expenses would need to be related to value added, or direct and indirect expenses to the larger quantity of total cost (or production value).[21] The Austrian expenditure data available does not include indirect expenses, but on the other hand it also goes beyond yearly direct expenses (by inclusion of total environmental investment data). Relating it to value added therefore gives numbers that overstate environmental control costs. Being restricted by the data, the most sensible measure appears to be to relate expenditures to production value (i.e. total cost) per industry sector. There is no estimate available for Austria on the indirect costs per industry sector that are needed but not included. On the other hand the data does include total investment, which strongly goes beyond the only item needed: yearly depreciation.

Table A.1 in the appendix gives the environmental control costs disaggregated for the 22 industry sectors. For matters of comparison also

---

20 If in a questionaire setting depreciation data on this issue is collected, for the data to be well interpretable it would be necessary to ask very detailed questions (especially what kind of depreciation method is used etc.). Thus, a trade off with the rate of respondance is very likely.

21 See section IV.2.1.2.1.

expenditures as a percentage of value added is given, though this (potentially strongly) overestimates ECC. The latter can serve, however, as a definite upper bound.

Results indicate that environmental control costs have risen slightly up to the early nineties, but that they still amount to a very low percentage of total costs. In 1985, the overall industry average was at 1.53% and had reached 2.10% in 1991.

Varying strongly across sectors implies that in particular sectors ECC are of much larger importance. They reach the highest value in the petroleum industry with 7.44% (up from 4.03% in 1985), which, however is a strongly protected industry; thus direct trade effects are unlikely. Indirect effects via other sectors at first glance seem very likely, but considering the special energy price agreements with industries demonstrates that this rather affects consumers directly, and hardly creates competitive disadvantage for industrial production.

All other sectors so far remain below a 5% cost share, albeit three sectors come close to this level. Chemicals, paper production and leather production show ECC in the range of 4.3 - 4.9%, ferrous metals, gas and heating, foundries and wood processing show them between 3.1 and 3.8, and stone and ceramics at 2.7%. The other sectors have ECC in the 0 - 2 percent range.

For matters of cost factor comparison, the relevant magnitudes will differ across sectors and mainly concern labor and capital cost. For trade considerations, some reference is given by the average Austrian tariff rate, currently at 4.9%.[22] Tariff rates only differ somewhat across sectors, but more so within sectors, rising with the degree of product processing. Therefore the available disaggregation of ECC is not sufficient to calculate direction and size of the gap between tariff rate and ECC explicitly for each product group. However, comparing sectorally ECC with the tariff rates at the product group level as specified in Breuss and

---

22 Breuss and Stankovsky (1988), p. 56; data refers to 1985.

Stankovsky (1988) indicates that for most product groups protection by import tariffs is effectively stronger than a potential competitive disadvantage due to ECC can amount to. Only for products of a low degree of product processing in the basic industries do ECC outweigh protection by import tariffs.

3.2. International Competitiveness in Industries with Strict Environmental Regulation

Direct conclusions on industry competitiveness from only the comparison of ECC across countries may be misleading. First, because the data is not homogenous across countries. But more importantly, because direct (and indirect) ECC are only one effect of environmental regulation. Full analysis would need to include all the (direct economic, mostly dynamic) benefits pointed out above which are not covered by them.

Thus a look at the actually observed trade flows - in the presence of environmental regulation - will give the more comprehensive overall conclusions on competitiveness. The standard hypothesis is that Austria, with its internationally comparatively strict environmental regulation level, will experience competitive disadvantage in those sectors that are subject to environmental control.

To determine the competitive export position of individual industry sectors the literature uses the indicator of relative world market share (RWS) of the products of this sector.[23] This index acknowledges that when measuring the export strength (and thereby international competitiveness in products) using the absolute export levels is inadequate as they depend on both size and openess of an economy. The RWS therefore relates the world market share of particular product groups to the overal world market share the country has. An $RWS_{i,j} > 1$ indicates that a country is specialized in exports in the sector j. An $RWS_{i,j} < 1$ indicates that within the exports of country i sector j's exports are underrepresented, thus that the country is not specialized in this sector.

[23] For a detailed discussion see Schumacher (1988).

$$RWS_{i,j} = \frac{e_{i,j} / \sum_{i=1}^{m} e_{i,j}}{\sum_{j=1}^{n} e_{i,j} / \sum_{i=1,j=1}^{m,n} e_{i,j}}$$

with $e_{i,j}$ denoting exports of country i in product group j.

First we need to select environmentally regulated sectors and obtain their export shares across countries. An extensive data source in this respect is supplied by Low and Yeats (1992). On the three-digit SITC level they identify 40 product groups as being related to high ECC and give trade flows for these goods for the period 1965-1988 for 109 countries. Umweltbundesamt (1993) calculated on this basis the respective RWS for the aggregate of these high ECC products for 20 major trading nations. The results are given in Table 4.3.

A potential limitation of Low and Yeats (1992) is that, not having available other country's ECC on a detailed level, they assume that the products connected with high ECC in their production in the U.S. are also the ones connected with high ECC in other countries. Checking the product groups reveals, however, that this assumption holds for Austria.[24]

With an RWS of 1.57 Austria actually shows, contrary to standard belief, an export specialization in environmentally heavily regulated industries. Of these exports 28% belong to the group of ferrous metals, 22% are paper manufactured products.[25] In contrast, other export oriented nations are much less specialized in these goods, even though some of them have lower regulation levels. E.g., the US (0.67), Taiwan (0.64), Korea (0.75) and Japan (0.52), whereas the Nordic countries Sweden (2.1) and Finland (3.27), to whom a high level of environmental awareness is generally attributed, reach highest specialization in these strictly regulated product groups. Germany, also showing rather strict standards, is in fact the largest exporter of these products in the world in absolute terms.

[24] Low and Yeats include ferrous metals, nonferrous metals, refined petroleum, metal manufacturing and paper manufacturing, and thus all sectors that show ECC above 3% in Austria in their base year 1988.

[25] Low and Yeats (1992), p. 95.

Table 4.3. Relative World Market Share in Environmentally Strictly Regulated Industry Sector Goods, 1988

Country	world market share [%]	RWS
Germany	11,9	1,00
USA	7,4	0,67
Canada	6,6	1,52
France	5,7	0,93
Belgium-Luxemburg	5,4	1,50
Netherlands	5,3	1,29
Japan	4,9	0,52
United Kingdom	4,5	0,90
Italy	4,2	0,88
Sweden	4,0	2,10
Finland	2,6	3,27
Soviet Union	2,2	1,85
Brazil	2,1	1,55
Austria	1,8	1,57
Spain	1,8	1,17
South-Korea	1,7	0,75
Taiwan	1,6	0,64
Norway	1,6	1,74
Australia	1,5	1,26
Switzerland	1,5	0,71

Source: UBA (1993), p. 92.

The results qualify arguments of competitive disadvantage due to strict Austrian environmental regulation, often cited in the discussion. They indicate that cost differences in environmental regulation to other countries are not so large that they would threaten Austrian competitiveness in highly regulated industries.

Insofar as "subsidized" production is concerned, one could argue that export flows do not represent true market competitiveness. But even if the complete ferrous sector is excluded from the analysis, Austria still shows an RWS above 1.

3.3. Environmental Goods and Services Industries

One economic sector that has a special relationship to national environmental regulation, the environmental goods and services industries, merits seperate treatment. For this sector it is generally considered that early and strict domestic environmental regulation enhances the foreign competitive position. Environmental regulation raises domestic demand in this sector and therefore production experience. For those goods and services that are later demanded also by other countries, such early experience is very likely to create comparative advantage for domestic production.

While this line of thought has been explored earlier with the *theoretical* concepts of economic geography,[26] in this section it is the empirical content of it for Austria that is our interest. The findings will be of particular relevance as this market is considered *the* growth market of the 90s. For example, EC authorities defined the target level of environmental investments to double within the first half of the 90s.[27]

For the environmental goods and services industries we also find, as for other sectors, some market segments that already have become standardized technologies, especially so in the end-of-pipe technology area. These segments are characterized by intensive price-competition. To a larger extent, however, Legler et al. (1992) in their study on high technology, consider environmental technology, being a very new area, as particularly research intensive. The development of new technologies in this field can rapidly change any competitive position that seemed established. For the future this stronger importance of non-standardized technologies will be even further enhanced as environmental responses increasingly switch from end-of-pipe approaches to preventive environmental protection and integrated technologies (that lower emission by changing the production process itself).

To date, it is mainly international market experience in end-of-pipe technologies we can observe empirically. We shall select two areas of air pollution regulation where Austria is known for its - in international comparison - very rigid standards: SO_2 emissions and organic pollutant emissions (in particular dioxine) from large combustion facilities.[28]

---

26 See section IV.1.2.

27 Legler et al. (1992), p. 107.

28 Luftreinhaltegesetz für Kesselanlagen 1988, with the particular emission limits specified in the Luftreinhalteverordnung für Kesselanlagen, 1989.

Investigations with one of the major technology suppliers in these areas, Austrian Energy and Environment, lead to the following result.[29]

For desulfurization equipment environmental regulation indeed caused Austrian production to be among the worlds furthest advanced. However, to date, the most broadly used technology and particular focus of Austrian production, wet fluid gas desulfurization, already is considered fully developed, such that there are no further know-how advantages to be realised in this area. The SO_2 removal efficiency that currently produced Austrian equipment supplies is 97,5%. Higher efficiencies could be reached within the same technology, being only a matter of increase in energy and capital used. Wet fluid gas desulfurization is based on washing flue gases. Higher efficiencies involve an increase in washing layers and scrubbing slurry (the washing substance), requiring additional nozzles and pumps, and implying higher operating energy.

Export market success in desulfurization equipment is mainly a question of adjusting the technology for the specific needs of the demanding countries. A large market is currently evolving in Central and Eastern European countries, but also within some developing countries. For this group of countries the direction of adjustment is to reduce costs by a reduction of automatization, especially as such a switch to higher labor intensity hardly affects the desulfurization result. Cost reductions achievable by such adjustments are substantial. Recently, for example, a not well adjusted Austrian offer for a facility in Turkey exceeded the offer of the cheapest supplier by 40%.

The case is different for the second example we are to look at, regulation of dioxine emissions. Such emissions were not regulated at all prior to 1989, when an emission limit of[30] 0,1 ng/m^3 went into effect in Austria (for new facilities immediately, for old facilites to catch up within a five year adjustment period). The regulation affects primarily waste incineration facilities. Emissions at that point had been in the range of 10

[29] Information was kindly supplied by Mr. Bärnthaler and Mr. Zechner, AE&E, at Graz and Vienna, June to September 1993.

[30] Specified for flue gases at 0 ^{0}C and 1.013 bar.

to 100 times higher, dependent on the particular processes used. This immediate increase in stringency caused particular switches in technology. It is remarkably that initially the main problem of equipment suppliers was not that of supplying the cleaner technology itself, but that of measuring the effectiveness of this technology as the methods of fume analysis available were not developed far enough to guarantee compliance. This has changed since.

Two other European countries, Germany and the Netherlands, followed Austrian regulation in this field immediately (while the absolute level is equivalent, Germany, however, only regulates daily averages, while Austria does so at the much stricter reference of half hour averages). This current regulation pattern across Europe determines export experiences. For Austrian Environment and Energy the major part of equipment production is indeed exported, with a strong increase since the introduction of the regulation in 1989 ("step function"). The export flows to date are almost exclusively to the two other countries with comparable regulation levels, Germany and the Netherlands. Regulation in other countries is at levels that imply the use of much simpler technologies. Current European guidelines are at a level that does not necessitate a switch to advanced technologies as supplied by the strict regulating countries. However, the simpler technologies cause larger quantities in remaining wastes. If costs for their dumping or treatment increase this would also increase the chances for cleaner technologies. Either such a cost increase or an increase in regulation stringency per se in other countries would be necessary to cause Austrian exports to expand beyond Germany and the Netherlands.

Also, the supply of the technology is determined by the European regulation pattern. It is especially German suppliers that Austrian producers are in strong competition with. Effectively, in high technology markets, it is a few suppliers who divide the market amongst themselves. That Austrian suppliers are in this group is due to the stringent Austrian domestic environmental regulation.

For both examples, desulfurization and the control of dioxine emissions, the actual employment and production effect is primarily in the engineering sector. Mechanical production has been never been really focused on domestically, but is mainly done abroad. For high technology this is due to agreements that require certain rates to be produced at foreign sites. For simpler parts, which are not affected by these restrictions, it is mainly the cost gap that determines their production mainly in Eastern and Central Europe. The engineering and maintainance sector, however, amount to a major part in the environmental goods and services industries, which will be pointed out shortly in empirical terms.

After the more detailed discussion of two examples that elucidate the particular micro-causations, we shall now turn to the aggregate development of this sector in Austria, more precisely to its trade performance.

First we shall employ RWS-analysis for this particular sector. As there are no seperate statistics on a clearly defined environmental sector, compromises in data use are necessary. Legler et al. (1992) use SITC III data on the five digit level to select environmentally relevant product groups. Only some product groups are clearly attributable to the environmental sector. Problems occur especially in noise protection, where the share of construction is high, and in the trade of simpler product categories, where goods can be used for environmental purposes, but also for other objectives (e.g. pumps). Legler et al. (1992) compromise on analysing a group of goods that *can* be used for environmental purposes (potential oriented analysis). For the year 1989 their study shows RWS values for Austria as stated in table 4.4 (see next page). They decide for a logarithmic scale; therefore in their results postive values indicate strong specialization whereas negative ones indicate a weak one.[31]

In particular in waste water treatment and air pollution reduction Austria indeed experiences foreign trade specialization. For waste treatment, 1989 was the year of the introduction of the major new regulation, results in

[31] They use the natural logarithm of the RWS index as defined earlier, and scale it by multiplication by 100.

Table 4.4. Relative World Market Shares for Austrian Environmental Goods and Services Industries, 1989

	world market share [%]	RWS
waste treatment	1,5	-9
waste water treatment	2,5	41
air	2,7	49
measuring and control technology	1,3	-27
total	2,1	23

Source: Legler et al. (1992), p. 113.

this segment are therefore no longer represenative. For measuring and control technologies Austria did not experience specialization. At the overall level for environmental goods and services Austria ranks fourth among OECD countries in trade specialization as table 4.5. indicates. Two other small open economies with high stringency levels in selected areas, Denmark and Switzerland, but remarkably also Italy experience stronger specialization in this goods category.

Table 4.5. RWS-Values in Environmental Goods and Services Industries for OECD Countries, 1989

Country	RWS	Country	RWS
Denmark	53	Netherlands	-38
Switzerland	42	Ireland	-54
Italy	30	Norway	-58
Austria	23	Belgium	-61
Germany	20	Canada	-85
United Kingdom	19	Australia	-104
USA	9	Greece	-113
Sweden	2	New Zealand	-135
Japan	-8	Portugal	-137
France	-10	Turkey	-159
Finland	-15	Iceland	-376
Spain	-17		

Source: Legler et al. (1992), p. 113.

As considerations at the example level above have indicated, however, further caution is necessary in interpreting this data. In the environmental goods and services sector there is also strong cross-hauling among countries. These simultanous import flows also have to be considered when conclusions are to be drawn for the actual comparative advantage. While the RWS index measures export specialization, it does not measure how well domestic production can hold its position in *domestic* markets relative to imports. For the evaluation of comparative advantage in both export and import markets the most broadly used measurement is the index of revealed comparative advantage (RCA).[32]

$$RCA_{i,j} = \frac{e_{i,j} / i_{i,j}}{\sum_{j=1}^{n} e_{i,j} / \sum_{j=1}^{n} i_{i,j}}$$

with $e_{i,j}$ representing the exports of country i of the goods category j and $i_{i,j}$ representing the respective imports.

Legler et al. (1992) have calculated the RCA values for the environmental goods and services industries for the OECD countries for the year 1989. Again they use the logarithm of the RCA index as defined here, and scale it by multiplication by 100.

Table 4.6. Revealed Comparative Advantage for Austrian Environmental Goods and Services Industries, 1989

	RCA
waste treatment	9
waste water treatment	13
air	47
measuring and control technology	-16
total	14

Source: Legler et al. (1992), p. 111.

The results indicate that Austria indeed experiences revealed comparative advantage in the environmental goods and services sector. As with export specialization, comparative advantage is also strongest in water treatment and air pollution abatement equipment, while there is revealed disadvantage in measuring and control technologies.

32 For a detailed discussion see Schumacher (1988).

The Austrian rank among the OECD countries, however, for comparative advantage is lower than it was found above for export specialization. The lead is again taken by Denmark, now followed by the US, Italy, Japan and Switzerland, Germany and the UK. Austria is placed eigth before France to complete the list of countries that experience comparative advantage. The remaining OECD countries experience disadvantage.

Table 4.7. RCA-Values in Environmental Goods and Services Industries for OECD Countries, 1989

Country	RCA	Country	RCA
Denmark	63	Netherlands	-26
USA	61	Finland	-30
Italy	55	Belgium	-37
Switzerland	46	Norway	-62
Japan	46	Canada	-102
Germany	40	Greece	-114
United Kingdom	17	New Zealand	-117
Austria	14	Australia	-121
France	4	Portugal	-122
Spain	-9	Turkey	-167
Sweden	-10	Iceland	-352
Ireland	-13		

Source: Legler et al. (1992), p. 111.

Summarizing, for the trade experience in the environmental goods and services industries respective technologies have to be distinguished as to whether they are already standardized or not. For standardized technologies export success depends on the ability to make technologies appropriate for the demanding country (especially the degree of automatization). For non-standardized technologies the large research component makes shifts in comparative advantage among countries very likely. Countries introducing environmentally strict regulation early enhance their chances for comparative advantage substantially. Empirical analysis of trade flows reveals that Austria to date in fact experiences comparative advantage as well as export specialization in the environmental goods and services industries.

3.4. Criteria for Further Empirical Analysis

The Austrian data presented so far gives a good snapshot of the current situation. For an analysis of even more substantial environmental policy, as is and will need to be discussed in the years ahead, however, a much more elaborate in-depth analysis is required.

For this, we can draw our lesson from both the recent theoretical studies and the international empirical studies undertaken and commented on in the two previous sections 1 and 2.

From the theoretical approaches it became evident that for those sectors that can be characterised by product differentiation, various opposing effects of unilaterally more stringent environmental policy can be observed. Considerations of an immediate production cost disadvantage are confronted with local market competion effects, strategic behavior and triggered innovation, each of them often working to counterbalance the initial disadvanatge. The net effect easily can be a reversed one. Models in this category so far, however, heavily depend on parameter specification, and are therefore only possible for partial analysis.

What is much more in current discussion is the other category of products, homogenous products. There the competitive disadvantage effects are much more crucial. Especially when substantial whole economy-wide environmental regulation is considered, it is these effects that are given most weight in political discussion. For the case of Austria, this is even more so, as one of its major characteristic is its large basic industry sectors.

From the considerations stated under "limitations of recent international empirical studies" a threefold conclusion arises. First, in measuring ECC, the indirect costs are substantial and should be considered to get reasonable results. Second, for studying the effect of environmental policy on trade, historical data alone does not allow adequate predictions regarding future developments. Third, to the degree possible, analysis needs to also include benefits that come with environmental regulation (directly and indirectly).

On the basis of these considerations both the subject and the methodology of the subsequent empirical study are chosen.

The emphasis currently being on the direct competitive effects of substantial environmental policy, the subject is a whole-economy analysis. An attempt can be made to get a quantitative handle on the benefits of environmental regulation. For the two other requirements, inclusion of indirect costs and allowance of a medium term forecast model, as methodological device computable general equilibrium analysis turns out to be best suited. Preceding the particular Austrian model this method will first be introduced in detail in the next chapter.

V

MODELING THE ENVIRONMENT-ECONOMY INTERACTION FOR AUSTRIA IN A TRADE-FOCUSED COMPUTABLE GENERAL EQUILIBRIUM FRAMEWORK

1. The Method of Computable General Equilibrium Modeling

1.1. Computable General Equilibrium Modeling for Environmental Policy Analysis

To analyze the impacts of human economic action and policy on the environment, a very broad range of tools has been developed, especially within the last two decades and within both the fields of economics and ecology. Mankind's living conditions are increasingly influenced by the state of the environment; not surprisingly the interest in how this state of the environment is affected by mankind has increased substantially.[1]

Out of this range of tools the current study picks Computable General Equilibrium Modeling for a number of reasons, which shall be stated at

[1] Bundesministerium für Umwelt (1993), Ökonomisch-Ökologische Modellbildung, provides an extensive overview of the literature that emphasizes the economic analysis in this interlinkage, compares approaches available and evaluates potential applications for Austria.

the very beginning. A comprehensive critical evaluation of the merits and limitations of this approach will be given after an overview of the characteristics of this method has been provided, the specific model has been constructed and simulation results have been obtained. At that point the evaluation will be most meaningful for the reader, and therefore the last section of this chapter is committed to this task in a fully detailed manner.

The choice of CGE-modeling involves certain implicit presuppositions. As we will see, for a broad range of questions connected to environmental policy these same concepts are crucial for analysis. Similarly, they are seen as being central for trade policy analysis. These understandings are the basis for a fruitful CGE application for the matter at hand - environment and trade.

First, and most evidently, in CGE modeling there is the understanding that prices matter. A CGE model generates a set of prices that are consistent with "equilibrium" in an economy. When (environmental) policy is introduced a new set of prices results. These prices, in turn, determine the level of production, the new sectoral structure, the level of income and the amount and direction of foreign trade flows - the variables we are ultimately concerned with. The use of CGE analysis therefore implies the belief that prices are important. This concept is similarly found in the environmental discussion. Aside from the more long term (but also in that time frame more appropriate) concerns about education and changes in societies´ value system, most immediate environmental policies in a decentralized decision framework aim ultimately at changing relative prices. In the discussion of foreign trade flows there is even longer experience with the effects of price changes caused by tariffs or export subsidies.

Second, there is the understanding that interactions matter. Otherwise a partial model would be much more appropriate. Environmental policy in particular is one area that affects the economy on a very fundamental level; it usually causes complex second-order ("feed-back") effects, that sometimes even outweigh first-order effects that would be considered alone in partial analysis. CGE modeling, by its disaggregated structure and allowance for changes in the material flows that link economic sectors, inherently takes account of all feedback effects. Each feedback effect does not need to be specified explicitely. The idea, rather, is that once the new economic equilibrium has been reached, prices and quantities have had to adjust such that all feed-back effects have been completed and are reflected by the final result.

Third is the understanding that economic structure matters. Structure means, for example, the size of individual sectors of domestic production or the share of foreign trade in GDP. Primarily in the development and trade area many CGE studies have focused on the importance of the economic structure in determining the effects of policy, and even more so, the effects of external shocks. For example, the effects that fluctuations in raw material world prices have on an economy, depend very much on the sectoral weights in that economy. For environmental policy analysis the notion of structure is similar with a twofold implication. At the outset, it involves a difference in economic costs of environmental policy depending on the original structure of an economy (e.g. the share of basic industries). Additionally, CGE modeling results in conclusions on how the structure of the economy will look once environmental policy has been carried out. This is of both theoretical and political importance. For theory it tells where the structural change of industrialization of the last two hundred years will tend to if environmental constraints are begun to be acknowlegded. Politically it informs in what sectors resistance to such intended environmental policies is particularly likely to be encountered.

As mentioned, the CGE approach is one in a range of tools of policy analysis. Its place may be defined better by comparing it with two alternative "bordering" tools, econometric macro-models and system-dynamic models.

The CGE approach has its foundation in economic theory in common with econometric modeling. In comparison, the CGE approach focuses on structural analysis and causal mechanisms at work due to a policy change, but cannot be used to make unconditional projections or forecasts. The latter is the domain of econometric macroeconomic models, that are disaggregated *temporally*, and rely heavily on lagged endogenous variables to capture expectations and frictions in the economy. Often, however, such (closed-form) macro-modeling makes tracking down causal mechanisms impossible, which is a strength CGE modeling supplies.

It shares this strength with system-dynamic modeling to some degree. System-dynamic modeling also focuses on the importance of indirect effects, but is based on a large number of "cause and effect circles", and not on an aggregate theoretical framework. System-dynamic models originated in the technical sciences[2], have since been applied in the social sciences as well[3], but as there is no economic theory involved, results cannot be traced back to it. They allow for an *explicit* modeling of all (also feedback) effects, which is not available in CGE modeling, but lack the economic (theory) foundation that CGE modeling provides.[4]

Finally, for the economic profession´s progress in policy analysis, there is an important part CGE modeling plays, which is - at first glance - often hidden behind a load of criticism concerning details employed by this method. In a CGE model all the assumptions and empirical parameters are specified explicitely on a very detailed level. No question, there may be large disagreements on the particular assumptions chosen. However, this can be a starting point for constructive debate that can focus on these particular behavioral assumptions, a particular sector, or a particular set of parameter values. In that way "disagreements and differences in policy recommendations can be traced back to specific behavioral assumptions, empirical estimates, or fundamental differences in normative goals"[5] and help to structure the discussion. This, and *not* an interpretation of results to be accurate to two decimal places, is the true value of the model. As

---

2 For an introduction see for example Forrester (1968), Principles of Systems.

3 In natural resource discussion most prominent: Meadows et al (1972), The Limits to Growth, and Meadows and Meadows (1992), The New Limits to Growth.

4 This became particularly evident in the discussion of "The Limits to Growth", as the study did not take account of input substitution effects due to price changes and resource scarcity triggering technical and structural change.

5 Dervis, de Melo and Robinson (1982), p.2.

two life-time scholars of this tradition condense it in the latest comprehensive CGE-survey[6]:

> The virtue of using applied general equilibrium models is that, once constructed, they yield a facile tool for analyzing a wide range of possible policy changes. Such analyses generate results that either yield an initial null hypothesis, or challenge the prevailing view. It may be that subsequently the conclusions of the model are rejected as inappropriate; the assumptions may be considered unrealistic, errors may be unearthed, or other factors may undermine confidence in the results. But there will be situations in which the modeler and those involved in the policy discussion process will have gained new perspectives as a result of using the model. In our opinion, this is the virtue of the approach, the reason why we believe its use in the policy process will spread further than the applications we report [in 1992, K.S.].

1.2. Basic Characteristics of a Computable General Equilibrium Model

1.2.1. Idea and Model Structure

CGE modeling is an approach that tries to further develop one of *the* fundamental concepts of economics, namely to grasp the complex interdependent relationships among decentralized actors in an economy by considering the actual outcome to represent a "general equilibrium". Dating back to Walras, it was formalized by Arrow and Debreu[7], and has subsequently been extended - parallel to the development of numerical solution algorithms - in order to be employed for practical empirical policy analysis. CGE modeling is thereby not meant to substitute for theory, but to build a logical complement, for the mutual improvement of both.

[6] Shoven and Whalley (1992), p.4.

[7] Arrow and Debreu (1954).

A CGE model is specified in the form of a list of equations, each of which can be classified under one of three categories:

(a) equilibrium conditions

(b) behavioral equations

(c) budget constraints.

Since the last aspect is uniformly shared by all model builders consideration shall start with it. Both in a schematic sense and as an actual empirical basis for a CGE model the best way to determine the budget constraints is the construction of a Social Accounting Matrix (SAM) of the economy. It combines data and concepts of two basic accounting systems of an economy, the input-output Table and the system of national income accounting. The reader interested in the construction of a SAM in more depth may turn to Appendix 3. The SAM specifies the constraints of income and expenditure-equality for each productive sector, each class of household, and the government. The SAM also specifies the macroeconomic budget constraints: the foreign balance and the domestic financial balance equilibrating investment and savings in the so called capital account. Due to Walras' Law it can be shown that when goods market equilibrium is introduced as well, one budget constraint can be dropped without loss of information.

The behavioral equations concern (b.1) the consumption behavior of the households, derived from the specification of their utility function; (b.2) the producer behavior of profit maximization and specification of the market structure, mostly perfect competition; (b.3) export demand; (b.4) import demand; (b.5) intermediate demand and (b.6) investment demand.

Most central here is producer behavior, because, based on the specification of production functions, it determines the link between factor markets, sectoral output, factor prices and goods prices. Household behavior makes final consumption endogenous in the model. The treatment of exports and imports opens many possibilities, it therefore will be covered below when the foreign sector is discussed in detail. Intermediate demand is mostly based on fixed input-output coefficients. The model employed in the current study will follow this path as well, except for the energy sectors, so that intermediate energy input will become flexible (allow for substitution between forms of energy, capital and labor). Investment in all static models represents only a demand category in the period of investment, it is assumed that it is not yet capacity effective in that period. Employing an investment demand coefficient matrix the investment per sector i can be translated to (investment) demand of goods from sector j.

Finally, the equilibrium conditions concern all markets, goods markets and factor markets. They ensure equilibrium of supply and demand by price adjustment. This closure is the distinctive strength of CGE modeling, because together with the budget constraints it causes the implicit inclusion of all indirect effects. The price the policy analyst pays is the fact of a model always characterized by full-employment. This could be avoided by various ad hoc assumptions, for example by fixing sectoral factor supply and factor price minima, but such assumptions are always set exogenously, factor unemployment is never created endogenously.

1.2.2. Time Horizon, Comparative Static and Dynamic Models

Full factor employment and market equilibria point out the time frame CGE analysis applies to. Time needs to be "long enough" to allow for market adjustment after policy change or an external shock. What "long enough" means can most importantly be governed by the behavioral parameters used, in particular elasticity of substitution parameters - the higher they are set the longer the time range the analysis applies to.

Particular features of CGE-modeling, however, make it mainly suggestive for what in economics is generally called "medium term analysis". For the short term, some aspects would be critical that are not the focus of CGE analysis: (1) Specific technical options and costs of change would need to be modeled, (2) the shift of factors between sectors usually is accompanied by (temporal) unemployment and (3) in the short term money matters. The first two have already been dealt with. With respect to monetary analysis, by the nature of CGE models within the Walrasian tradition they assume money to be neutral and are only concerned with relative prices, a characteristic that is relevant only for medium and long term analysis[8].

For analysis of the very long term, so to say at the other end of the potential time frame, the *inherent* modeling of time behavior becomes critical and has to be considered. In this respect a distinction has to be made between the two possible CGE approaches, comparative static and dynamic analysis.

In comparative static analysis the model is first solved for a base year the empirical data of which is available. Next a base case solution is determined for a future point in time, using a set of parameters governing time behavior, such as sectoral productivity changes and factor supply growth rates. Third, this base case solution is compared to counterfactual solutions of the model using different sets of policy parameters. The longer the time horizon, the more comparative static analysis will have problems arguing for the particular choice of time behavior parameters.

To avoid this problem, the development has recently gone towards intrinsic modeling of the dynamics within CGE models. In early approaches along this line the period equilibria were simply connected by the evolution of capital endowment, which in turn depends on savings behavior[9]. This being still unsatisfactory, as it does not model actual intertemporal optimization of agents, CGE modeling was combined with

---

[8] Especially in development economics often behavior with respect to inflation (e.g investment despite hyperinflation) requires non-neutrality of money and therefore has been introduced in various models. For a study in the European context focusing on this aspect see Capros (1992), constructing a European multicountry CGE with explicit modeling of the monetary sector.

[9] Fullerton, King, Shoven and Whalley (1981) and Fullerton, Shoven and Whalley (1983) are the two first approaches of that kind, analyzing tax policy. For an Austrian environmental policy application see Farmer and Steininger (1994), expanding the model presented in this report for dynamic analysis.

overlapping generation theory[10]. This, however, also involves substantial trade-offs. Intertemporal optimization in every period increases the dimensionality of the problem substantially, but also the data demand for values that are much more difficult to derive from empirical observations. Therefore dynamic models so far have to acknowledge strong constraints either in sectoral disaggregation or in model specification. Moreover, as Auerbach and Kotlikoff (1987) show, such models are very unstable. Their behavior is strongly sensitive to the choice of those parameters that still need to be set exogenously - in the Auerbach and Kotlikoff modeling this being the discount rate and the amount of terminal capital (the transversality condition).

Considering these limitations of intrinsically forward looking CGE models, even they can hardly be considered to be true long-term analysis intstruments, but rather apply for medium term analysis, as does the comparative static approach.

The current study in section 2 for its Austrian model chooses a comparative static approach in order to (a) have a fuller picture of intra-period relationships while (b) being not restricted too strongly in the choice of the model specification, such that especially a rich substitution between input factors (the critical part in analyzing environmental policy) is allowed for. "Dynamic" aspects come into the model also, by the specification of the time-development of the main framework conditions for the economy. They, however, need to be derived exogenously to the model.

1.3. The History of Computable General Equilibrium Modeling and its Major Applications

CGE modeling by now has developed very broadly in terms of policy questions analysed and has divided into various traditions also in a

---

[10] Auerbach and Kotlikoff (1983) and Ballard (1983) started this tradition. For a survey of intertemporal models in the Shoven-Whalley tradition see Preira and Shoven (1988). For a dynamic optimizing model on Austria see Keuschnigg and Kohler (1993).

technical sense. This is the reason why it is not easy to point to a standard comprehensive survey; there are virtually none. In the last decade quite a few excellent survey articles have been published, but because of the field´s broadness they focus either on CGE models analysing a particluar policy area, or they give an overview on modeling experience within a particular tradition. For the first category of policy-specific surveys, those that are of environmental and trade relevance will be reviewed in the next section. For the latter category mainly five major traditions within CGE modeling can be distinguished. A respective detailed overview of each of them is provided by Shoven and Whalley (1992), Dervis, de Melo and Robinson (1982), Ginsburgh and Waelbroeck (1981), Jorgenson (1984) and Dixon et al. (1982).

The only exception regarding comprehensive surveys seems to be Bergman (1990). Taking his work as a foundation, and including information collected at various lectures given by the main representatives of the other traditions, the author considers it useful to tackle the task of a brief categorization of CGE modeling traditions in order to give the reader an organizational scheme for the enormous amount of CGE studies, quite a few of which will be cited in the course of this chapter.

1.3.1. The Johansen Approach

In the profession, the dissertation work of Leif Johansen, published in 1960, is generally considered the original inspiration and starting point of numerical general equilibrium analysis. His thesis "A multi-sectoral study of economic growth" was intended to contribute to the explanation of the development of resource allocation in the Norwegian economy over time. The major differences from later CGE modeling were the restriction to a single household sector (lifted in later models for the focus of income distribution analysis), basically a closed economy (with exports and imports set exogenously, lifted in all trade analysis models) and full (log)linearization of the model specification. The last characteristic was simply due to the fact that in 1960 only algorithms for numerical solution of linear problems of this dimensionality were available.

The further development of solution techniques in the last three decades was both the very foundation of further advances in CGE model building and also represents one line along which different traditions can be distinguished. Therefore it shall be surveyed next.

1.3.2. The Development of Solution Techniques

Within solution techniques it is helpful to distinguish solution strategies and solution algorithms.[11] A solution strategy concerns the way a set of simultanous nonlinear equations is established numerically, such that the solution will give all endogenous variables. A solution algorithm refers to the computational technique for actually solving this system.

1.3.2.1. Solution Strategies

Johansen's (1960) original solution strategy was to reduce the model to a set of log-linear equations (linear in growth rates) in all endogenous variables, such that he could solve the system by algorithms applicable for linear models. Later, solution algorithms were developed by which non-linear equation systems could also be solved. Since then, solution strategies mainly concern the sequence of checking for market equilibria in all markets.

For open economy models Dervis, de Melo and Robinson distinguish two such main solution strategies.[12] Comparing them will also show how model specification, solution strategy and solution demand relate to each other.

Open economy models consist centrally of factor markets, product markets and the foreign exchange market. One can, first, think of starting with a guess of factor prices, which, given sectoral cost functions and assuming perfect competition, will give sectoral cost prices. If, additionally, constant return to scale technology is assumed, these cost prices are independent of the output level. Given the supplies of factors,

---

[11] This distinction follows Adelman and Robinson (1978).

[12] Dervis, de Melo and Robinson (1982), pp. 486ff.

total factor incomes can be derived. If (sectoral) product demand now is only dependent on this aggregate of total factor income, it can be readily derived and compared to sectoral supply. If there is excess demand in any product market, a new iteration is started with a different set of factor prices, until excess demand is zero. Adelman and Robinson (1978) refer to this strategy as "factor market strategy".

If, however, the model is specified with more detail, such that product demand also depends on either the structure of factor income or the structure of production (e.g. by governmental demand dependent on tax income, which in turn depends on the sectoral structure of production due to different sectoral tax rates), a much more demanding strategy has to be chosen. Then, a so called "product market strategy" is necessary, which starts out with a guess of product prices and the exchange rate. It concentrates first on factor markets until a set of factor prices is found that results in factor demands (derived from profit maximization given the product price guesses) that match factor supplies. This gives disaggregated factor income and production structure, from which household and government income can be derived. Next, at the second level in this strategy, sectoral product demands are calculated therefrom and are compared to the product supplies. If the two do not match in all markets, a new iteration is started with a different combination of product prices and exchange rate. Again, first the factor markets are brought into equilibrium and then product market equilibrium is checked. The solution demand of this latter strategy obviously is much larger and shows the trade-off between flexibility in model specification and the computational demand that results.

1.3.2.2. Solution Algorithms

Which solution algorithm then is applicable depends on the strategy chosen. Algorithms can be classified into

(a) Simple algorithms for log-linear systems
(b) Constrained maximization algorithms and
(c) Excess demand equation algorithms.

The first category dates back, as mentioned, to the original idea for solving economy-wide, general equilibrium models numerically by Johansen (1960) in linearizing the equation system. The advantage is the simplicity of the algorithm and the resulting cheapness of its application, especially relevant in large scale-models. The disadvantage lies in both the restriction on the model specification such that it can be linearized and the strong affection of results by approximation errors. These errors also increase with the magnitude of changes in the exogenous variables, as they influence growth *rates*. Johansens work was later refined substantially, first of all in the external sector, and is currently not only enjoying continued use in Norway, but Australian economic policy advising is also primarily based on a model in this tradition, the ORANI model.[13] The major advantage of this solution algorithm is, as mentioned, the allowance for large-scale specification. The ORANI model therefore can be used for very detailed analysis as it includes in its standard version more than 100 distinct classes of each of the following: producing sectors, domestically produced commodity types and (industry-specific) capital. For specific purposes it was further disaggregagted in the respective sectors[14], indicating a potential which is a *general* feature of CGE modeling. However, in other traditions the total disaggregation amount is comparatively limited, i.e. while one sector may be disaggregated the rest of the model has to be "re-aggregated".

The second class of algorithms, constrained maximization algorithms, represents a natural extension of linear programming models. They make the introduction of inequalitiy constraints very easy, but it is often not at all convenient to express the model in terms of all different actors and institutions. The mathematical features shown in Takayma and Judge (1971), two of the initial applications of this solution method are Goreux and Manne (1973) and Ginsburgh and Waelbroeck (1978).

The third category is the one most broadly used. Algorithms of this kind use excess demand equations directly and are applicable for solution

[13] For an introduction see Dixon et al. (1982).
[14] For example, in ORANI-MILK the dairy sector was disaggregated in detail.

strategies such as exemplified above. They again can be classified into three types: (1) based on fixed-point theorems, (2) based on a tatonnement process, and (3) based on gradients.

The first class, algorithms based on fixed point theorems, dates back to the seminal work of Scarf (1967, 1973). His work can also be considered the true trigger of the large spreading of CGE analysis beyond the Johansen linearization approach. In the development of economic theory the existence of the general equilibrium had been long proven. Abraham Wald (1934) gave the first rigorous proof of the existence of a solution for a system of simultanous equations and Arrow and Debreu (1954) proved this existence for the later reformulated problem of explicitely formalized independent agents optimizing behavior being compatible. These developments were important to show the consistency of the models, as they proved that there was an equilibrium, but did not supply any techniques in the finding of it numerically. For policy makers interested in the results of comparative static analysis, however, logical consistency of the models is only a prior necessity, but calculation of the equilibria the actual interest. The so called Scarf algorithm provides such a technique for finding the equilibrium as it guarantees convergence to it. By guaranteeing convergence it is, however, also very demanding. Basically it rests on a no-cycling procedure that implies that whenever the end result is not detailed enough, one has to start at the very beginning, and secondly initial guesses cannot be used, but the iterations have to be started at corner points.

Due to the time- and cost intensity of methods based on this algorithm, most model builders have moved away from it again, using kinds of Newton stepwise approaches, that actually cannot guarantee convergence, but are much faster and cheaper. So, the Scarf algorithm can be considered the breakthrough of a locked situation, when Arrow (1959) had proved that Tatonnement processes need not converge. Now, that there is an algorithm that guarantees convergence, economic model builders have returned to using algorithms that are practical, but do not necessarily converge. So the algorithms that are mainly used at present were available already in the early sixties, but were applied only after

Scarf´s work. The logic behind the use of such not necessarily converging algorithms is the argument that only comparatively small policy changes are generally analysed, for which these algorithms should make it possible to find the new equilibrium, but also the success of this method in practical experience over the last two decades.

What currently can be observed is something of a divide between the theory and application of CGE techniques. In theoretical work the first class of computational procedures based on fixed-point theorems is focused on, because it guarantees convergence, whereas in pratical applications the remaining two approaches, as surveyed below, are employed. They drop the no-cycling argument, which leads to substantial increases in speed. Theoretical work, based on the first kind of algorithm, is done very much within the tradition considered most "Walrasian", that can be labeled the Scarf-Harberger-Shoven-Whalley-tradition. In their practical work, however, this tradition also uses algorithms mainly of the third kind.

Algorithms based on a tatonnement process simply adjust the price in each sector in response to that sector's excess demand. This technique is implemented as a special version of the Gauss-Seidel iteration procedure (not requiring any evaluation of derivatives of the excess demand functions)[15]. It is therefore very easy to implement, and once the algorithm is "tuned" to the problem, also very efficient. However, such tuning of the algorithm requires the user´s full understanding of the algorithms and the models´ properties, such that it cannot be used as a "canned" program. Also the algorithm becomes very inefficient when there is a large number of market interactions in the model to be solved.

Therefore the algorithms used most widely today are of the third kind. They additionally use information supplied by the derivatives of the excess demand functions in determining the iteration step direction and size. As they are based on and sensitive to the determinant of the matrix of

[15] This algorithm is used in the original work of Adelman and Robinson (1978), Dervis (1975) and Dungan (1980) for example.

numerical derivatives, the Jacobian, they are often labeled "Jacobian algorithms". All traditions covered below use this kind of algorithm.

For a good overview of the Johansen-Dixon-type log-linearization approach, see - besides the original references - Bergman (1990). A comprehensive formal exposition of algorithms based on fixed point theorems is supplied by Shoven, Whalley and Wiegard (1992). Short introductions to Jacobian algorithms are supplied by Dervis, de Melo and Robinson (1982), appendix B, and Shoven, Whalley and Wiegard (1992), section 3.9.

1.3.3. A Classification of Current Traditions and Applications

As the overview on survey articles already indicated, five traditions in CGE modeling can be distinguished.

The tradition closest to Walrasian theory is associated with the names of Scarf, Harberger, Shoven and Whalley[16].

> Their models to a very large extent can be regarded as numerical counterparts of Walrasian general equilibrium theory. [...] Consequently, the numerical model has to be entirely consistent with an explicit theoretical model; incorporating ad hoc assumptions may make the model more 'realistic' but also difficult or impossible to interpret,

as Bergman (1990) characterizes this tradition. In terms of policy issues this tradition mainly focuses on public finance and trade analysis. Models are constructed such that policy changes can be evaluated in terms of both efficiency and income distribution effects. This tradition therefore basically represents applied welfare economics.

In the other field of major CGE application, development economics, deviations from pure Walrasian theory are given much more weight. Coming from the notion that especially developing economies cannot be well described by pure neoclassical theory, ad hoc assumptions are introduced into the models to make their behavior more realistic.

---

16 The probably still best survey is Shoven and Whalley (1984).

Theoretical proofs of equilibrium existence play almost no role. This tradition originates from economic-planning issues and input-output analysis. If a line of historical development of this tradition is drawn, it would lead from Walras directly to Leontief´s input-output models and then via Dantzig´s, Koopman´s and Chenery´s linear programming models to Adelman and Robinson (1978). Studies in this line are almost exclusively done by researchers connected in some way to the World Bank. Researchers in this so-called "neoclassical structuralist" tradition include Dervis, de Melo and Devarajan. A slightly different line within the development CGE applications is represented by Taylor, who introduces non-neutrality of money, and therefore his approach often is labeled "macro-structuralist".[17]

The root in Leontief's input-output analysis which characterizes this development tradition is shared by the oldest tradition, that was already dealt with above, and dates back to the linearization approach of Johansen and its later refinements.

The distinction separating the next line of research concerns the way parameter estimates for data not contained in the SAM are gained. For all of the above traditions this can be either done by "calibration" or, and this can be distinguished as a separate tradition, by econometric methods. In a very general form a CGE model can be specified as

$$F_i(Y_1, \ldots .Y_n; X, B, e) = 0 \qquad i = 1,2,\ldots .n$$

with Y_i representing a vector of endogenous variables, X a vector of exogenous variables, B a vector of m unknown parameters and e a vector of stochastic disturbances.

For calibration it is assumed that the analyst knows the right model fully and that the data of the base period is generated by it. In other words, all components of e are set to zero and the system is solved for the vector B on the basis of the base year (single) realization of Y_i and X. If B has a

17 For example, Sherman Robinson, courses on CGE modeling in 1991, 1992.

higher dimension than *Y*, a number equal to the difference m - n of parameters has to be gained from outside the available data, basically from other studies. This calibration method implies serious restrictions on the analysis, mainly by creating demand for a low number of exogenous parameters to be estimated (a low dimension of *B*), which primarily is reached by rather simple specifications of both preferences and technologies. In most applications they are based on either CES or Cobb-Douglas functional forms, as they have only a small number of parameters. Consequently the econometric tradition overcomes this problem by a stochastic specification of the model and by econometric estimation of the model parameters. But not only the time series data demand increases using this method, the dimensionality of the computational problem also increases strongly with higher disaggregation, so that it becomes the new constraint for this method. An alternative is to implement only submodels in stochastical specification and use them as building blocks in a general equilibrium model. The first example in this econometric CGE tradition was Hudson and Jorgenson (1975). Current work along this line is mainly done by Dale W. Jorgenson and his co-researchers.

Also with its historical origin in the World Bank is the fifth tradition, "activity analysis general equilibrium", that is primarily connected with Victor A. Ginsburgh and Jean L. Waelbroeck as well as with Alan S. Manne. Bergman (1990) considers it a "matter of definition whether models in this tradition should be regarded as a variant of CGE models or as an alternative to CGE models". This approach is based on linear programing models, but tries to avoid their inherent tendency toward switching state solutions, not by ad hoc assumptions, but by introducing restrictions based on economic theory, mainly resulting in piecewise linearized functions. In empirical terms this enables the construction of models based on actual engineering or other very detailed empirical data, whereas other traditions here only assume continuous substitution. Due to computational difficulties, however, it is likely that the major further developments will rather take place within the other four traditions.[18]

[18] For example, Bergman (1990), pp. 24-25, points out this direction.

1.4. Environmental Computable General Equilibrium Models

1.4.1. Overview

Besides the traditional areas of CGE application, trade, finance and development, first energy policy analysis gained importance, and building on it, more recently, environmental policy analysis.

There are surveys on energy and also resource CGE models: Bergman (1988) for energy applications and Devarajan (1988) for natural resource tax policy analysis in the development context. For environmental policy CGE analysis, however, there only a few issue mimeos exist, like Devarajan (1992) for the subset of developing country issues, but no surveys so far.

Looking at Bergman (1988) the two major conclusions he draws from the overview of major simulation results of *energy* policy studies are highly relevant for our purpose as well. First, he points out that the studies show that quite dramatic changes in long-run energy consumption patterns can take place without significant negative impact on economic growth (measured in traditional terms). Second, as similarly stated at the beginning of this chapter, he emphasizes the pedagogical value of CGE modeling "having the potential of changing prejudices about the functioning of the economy and thus of contributing to economically sound energy policies."[19]

With environmental policy discussion now increasingly concentrating on both significant damages and therefore *significant* emission reduction objectives, CGE modeling was the logical method of analysis to turn to. Substantial emission reduction will tend to have large effects on some or several sectors in the economy; the resulting shifts in relative costs are very likely to induce effects throughout the economy, namely general equilibrium effects that are not observable within partial models.

---

[19] Bergman (1988), p. 398.

The origin of this multisector environmental analysis dates back to Leontief's seminal (1970) article presenting a multisector input-output model that incorporated environmental externalities. Throughout the seventies and early eighties there was an active literature building on such input-output analysis to analyze pollution matters in a multisector interdependent framework.[20] But being unpleased with the relatively fixed economic structure in input-output-models that is due to the specification in terms of linear limitational production functions, multisector analysis was further developed to allow for better endogenous input substitution options, which lead to the construction of economy-wide environmental CGE models.

Compared to traditional CGE models the main extensions of environmental models are the distinction of a much larger number of (energy) input factors and - in many models - the explicit specification of pollution abatement possibilities, which is usually modeled within a separate "cleaning" sector in explicit (e.g. Robinson, 1990) or implicit terms (e.g. Bergman, 1991). Robinson (1990) supplies a brief theoretical introduction into the theoretical and empirical (functional) issues encountered, and also constructs a simple CGE model based on the stylized Leontief data.

Environmental CGE models by now, even though mainly developed within the last three years, already show such a broad range of application that it again appears to be very useful to try to categorize them.

Distinction criteria concern (1) the geographic and analytical scope: single country or region anaylsis versus multicountry analysis, (2) the main question focused on: economic cost of environmental regulation, inclusion of benefit analysis, and/or focusing mainly on income distributional aspects and (3) the set up of the model as static or intrinsically dynamic. Additionally, all aspects considered in distinguishing various CGE traditions apply, especially concerning the way parameters are gained, by calibration or estimation.

---

[20] For an overview see Schröder (1990), chapter 1.2.

Most often analysis is carried out within single country or single-region models, as they allow for a richer disaggregation of production sectors and households than multicountry models, but also from a practical point of view, as data collection and estimation is accomplished more easily, as it can be based on a single framework of national accounting. For intrinsically global or multicountry questions, such as analysing the effects of global environmental agreements, however, only multicountry analysis can give substantial helpful insights, as only there the quantities and prices which are then crucial are endogenized.

Single-country analysis itself is best classified by the thematic focus it has. A first and important question is the quantification of economic costs (mainly in terms of income growth reduction) of environmental regulation. Bergman (1990,1991) for Sweden, Schröder (1990), Conrad and Schröder (1991) for Baden-Württemberg, Jorgenson and Wilcoxen (1991) for the US are studies in this line.

But environmental policy is done because of the benefits it promises. Some studies, first covering environmental policy cost anaylsis, then also try to add rough calculations of (some) of its benefits to give a fuller picture and basis for policy decision. This on one hand can be introduced exogenously as in Glomsrod et al. (1991) and Brendemoen and Vennemo (1992), which estimate health benefits of Norwegian emission reduction and compare it to the CGE model cost results. But it also can be done intrinsically in the actual CGE model as Bergman (1993) shows. In his set up, pollution directly affects production negatively and also enters household utility function. Reducing emissions therefore has an intrinsic positive effect depicted in the model.

Bergman (1993), however, considers his results rather guesstimates highly dependent on weak benefit relationship data. The main value of the model at this initial stage is serving as a basis for getting started discussing such issues in more depth. A less disagreeable empirical data basis is built upon by another line of research showing that environmental policy cost estimates "of the first generation" were mostly too high even from a standard economic point of view. Nestor and Pasurka (1992, 1993a) model the interaction between the economy, environmental regulation and the sector providing environmental protection goods and services in a very detailed manner. They show for the Federal Republic of Germany that environmental policy leads to large positive impacts on output generated through purchases of pollution abatement equipment, this offsetting much of the traditional cost estimates.

A somewhat different focus is the analysis of distributional effects that environmental policy causes. By allowing for detailed household disaggregation (e.g. by income class) CGE analysis is highly appropriate for this purpose. For example, Stephan et al. (1992) show for Switzerland that due to distributional effects, political acceptability of a CO_2 tax will highly depend on the particular revenue redistribution scheme chosen.

Most of the single country models mentioned above are static: Bergman, Brendemoen and Vennemo, Glomsrod et al., Nestor and Pasurka, Robinson, and Stephan et al.. Dynamic models are Jorgenson and Wilcoxen, Schröder, and Conrad and Schröder.

The alternative main class of models is multicountry models. They usually require a group of a few researchers for construction but also maintainance. Currently there are two main multicountry global environmental models. One is maintained within the OECD, the GREEN model (Burniaux et al., 1992). Secondly, Whalley and Wigle (1991) developed a model that later was built upon in further studies: Piggot et al. (1991), Pezzey (1991), and Piggot and Whalley (1992). Both approaches are global models and contain country blocks. Both have been mainly used for global CO_2 policy questions, basically concerning income, growth and trade effects for the various country groups and as such also concerning the incentives to join agreements depending on the specific set up of the agreement.

1.4.2. Characteristics and Results of Recent Environmental CGE Studies

In order to exemplify possible approaches of environmental modeling in a CGE framework and the kind of results that are obtainable by the CGE method, distinctive recent studies shall be surveyed in more detail.

1.4.2.1. Single Country and Single Region Static Modeling

In the class of comparative static single country analysis, Bergman (1991) combines a range of features. Bergman´s objective is to study the structural and growth effects on the Swedish economy of emission reduction targets for SO_X, NO_X and CO_2, applying them within a time-frame of 15 years. Emissions in the model are both due to combustion (proportional to the use of fuels by industry sectors and households - relevant for all pollutants analysed) and to industry processes (proportional to sectoral output levels - relevant for SO_X, because here the amount emmitted depends heavily on the kind of process used). Total emissions can be reduced by means of seperate cleaning activities that are available to all sectors. Environmental policy is assumed to be implemented cost-effectively, and is thus simulated by a tradeable permits market.

Sweden being a small open economy, special emphasis is given to accurate foreign trade modeling. According to the respective foreign competitive position, economic sectors are aggregated into seven sectors, including two strongly exposed ones that are international price-takers, three sheltered sectors that show some international price setting power, and two non-trading sectors.

For the exposed sectors, which are also the most pollution intensive, the model allows for distinction between "old" production capital, available at the base year and not allowing for input-substitution, and "new" production capital. This is also an elegant way to cover technological progress in an intrinsically static model. In comparison, most other static studies neglect technical progress, whereas it is a major feature in dynamic analysis.[21]

For quite significant emission reduction targets (compared to unconstrained development, SO_X is reduced in the policy case by 44%, NO_X by 57% and CO_2 by 28%), the results show a reduction in yearly GDP growth from the base case of 2% to 1.7%. Benefits accruing are not estimated. The model is also used to analyze the effects of various levels of CO_2 emission reduction. Results indicate that only reduction levels of more than 20% (compared to the base case) cause significant general equilibrium and growth effects (for a constant emission level, a 30% reduction from the base case would be needed). At the time of model construction, a CO_2-tax of 25 Öre per kg was discussed in Sweden and later introduced, also on the basis of the results given by Bergman (1991). That tax level was estimated by the model to cause approximately a 25% reduction in CO_2 emissions and a yearly GDP growth reduction of 0.1%.

Boyd and Krutilla (1992) is interesting as their results for a large (and less foreign trade dependent) economy, the US, show the basic feature of sectoral counterbalancing shifts in CGE modeling very clearly. They analyse the impact of the SO_2 provisions in the 1990 Clean Air Act on the US economy (in the first phase, 1990-1995, a yearly emission reduction by 4 million tons for public utilities is intended). The objective is reached in the model by the introduction of a respectively high electricity tax. As there is no allowance for input substitution in public utility elctricity production (fixed coefficients are assumed), the cost results are upper bounds. Output in public utilites therefore has to shrink by 14%, which has significant effects on the sectors coal (-27%, as coal is the main input of public utilities), oil refinement (-2%) and services (-1,4%). As both demand and factor input have to shift to other sectors, there is also one sector with net growth on a significnat level: agriculture (+1%). Accordingly, factor prices adjust: labor and capital as the main inputs of public utilities get cheaper, the price of land as the main input in agriculture increases.

---

[21] See the overview on Jorgenson and Wilcoxen (1990) below.

Distinguishing six household income classes, they analyse the distributional effects, and show that for the lowest income class the rise in income due to land price appreciation (this income class being the main land holder) outweighs the reduction in other factor incomes. For all other income classes it is reverse, and real income shrinks for them.

Brendemoen and Vennemo (1992) focus on the distribution effect of environmental policy in much more detail, as they (a) base their study on distingusihing between 1500 representative households (that are available in the Norwegian consumer statistics) and (b) also include explicit benefits and their distribution on household categories. Their policy simulation case is that of a global climate convention (stabilizing CO_2 emissions by the year 2000 at the 1987 level, and thereafter allowing for a yearly increase of 0.6%), which enters the CGE model by its exogenously determined effects on the development of world prices for oil and coal. Rising energy prices reduce fuel use and emissions of various pollutants (nine are explicitely covered). The locally distinguished benefits of the climate convention accrue aside from health benefits derived directly from these emission reductions, also from reduced noise and traffic accidents, as the traffic volume reacts to the higher energy prices. The study indicates that there will be no significant distributional effects for the case of Norway. Lower income class welfare is mainly effected by the rise in fuel oil prices. For higher income classes the net welfare effect remains the same, as the welfare loss due to rising gasoline price increases, while the loss due to fuel oil price increase becomes less relevant.

Overall, the climate convention causes a reduction of yearly economic growth by 0.1%. CO_2 emmissions fall by 60%. The calculated simultanous reduction of other pollutants is used for a (lower bound) estimate of benefits, which amount to 80% of GDP-reduction.[22]

---

[22] While this study is unique in its detailed emphasis on benefit determination, the cost side is strongly dependent on assumptions about how the climate convention effects world oil and coal prices. Even though a major part of project work was put into that part, some of the assumptions still appear to remain arbitrary.

While Brendemoen and Vennemo analyse the effects of a global CO_2 convention on a national economy, for many pollutants the environmental problem itself is much more only a national or even an intra-country-regional one. How the CGE method can be adjusted to be applicable for the analysis of an environmental problem of mainly regional dimension is exemplified by Robinson et al. (1994), analysing air pollution in the Los Angeles Basin. The LA region is disconnected from the rest of the U.S. by assuming locally produced commodities to be imperfect substitutes for imported commodities, imported from both the rest of the U.S. and from foreign countries. Los Angeles also cannot be assumed to have its own currency, so its exchange rate is fixed with respect to the U.S., and the region´s own balance of trade is determined. Factor markets can be seen as linked to the rest of the U.S., with the wage determined exogenously and the LA labor market clearing by migration into and out of the region. Robinson et al. decide for the alternative approach of taking the labor supply in the region as given and to solve for the market clearing regional wage rate.

The environmental content of the analysis is to test the new approach to air pollution reduction in the Los Angeles basin, "Regional Clean Air Incentives Market" (RECLAIM), based on tradeable emission reduction credits.[23] The model accordingly is constructed in the spirit of Bergman's (1991) tradeable permits modeling. The particular characteristic of the Robinson et al. (1994) model is its treatment of abatement activities in a discrete manner based on sectoral technological data; it therefore merges CGE and activity anaylsis. Results indicate emission reduction levels that can be reached by relatively low emission charge levels: 50% reduction for NO_X, 25% for ROG and 35% for SO_X. At these reduction levels abatement possibilities are exhausted. Higher reduction objectives can only be achieved by structural change, thus at a considerably higher cost (and emission charges level). Model results indicate that for the emission charges to yield the above reduction objectives the costs of abatement to firms are relatively small and also the reduction in regional value added is small (of the order of 1 to 2%).

[23] See South Coast Air Quality Management District (1993).

1.4.2.2. Single Country Dynamic Modeling

For the intertemporal dimension - environmental regulation is very likely to involve significant changes in the formation of capital - Hazilla and Kopp (1990) employ a respectively constructed CGE model, dynamic and econometrically estimated. The objective being a determination of the social costs of the main U.S. environmental regulations, those mandated by the Clean Air and Clean Water Acts (1970 and 1972, recent ammendments), they base their study on time series data covering the pre- and post-regulation period and econometrically estimate the CGE model. A Base Case Scenario of no-regulation is compared with the actual development of the U.S. economy. The econometric approach is chosen to allow for very flexible functional forms, so that direct regulations in each of the 36 production sectors can be modeled on a solid micro-foundation using detailed environmental compliance engineering cost data to determine the sector-specific production cost functions.

The second distinctive feature of the model - the intertemporal modeling - is introduced by linking the current labor market to the next period´s capital stock. The current labor market situation determines household income, which in turn gives household savings. Set equal to investment, this determines the capital stock in the subsequent period.

Hazilla and Kopp mainly compare their results with standard U.S environmental cost estimates based solely on technical compliance cost. For the short run they show that the social regulation costs they are able to derive are much lower than private compliance cost estimates, as there are general equilibrium substitution effects towards clean sectors reducing compliance costs and towards leisure as the relative price of consumption increases. Dynamic social costs of environmental regulation, however, are, according to their analysis, higher than engineering compliance cost estimates. The relative price decrease of leisure causes more leisure consumption, therefore less income and less savings, which reduces capital formation. Output grows less than in the unregulated case. Considering this dynamic effect, their social cost estimate for the period 1981-1990 is higher by a factor 1.5 than EPA compliance cost estimates. Again, benefits are not compared with this cost estimate. While the dynamic aspects of capital formation are well analysed, given the assumption of the labor market-capital formation link to be the main important one, the issue of technical progress triggered by environmental regulation is not covered in the model. Rather the technological progress the U.S. has observed in the last twenty years under environmental regulation is taken as given for both scenarios, and thus assumed to be independent of environmental regulation.

The problem of regulation dependent technological progress is endogenized by Jorgenson and Wilcoxen (1990), also within a dynamic and econometrically estimated model. Starting from the result of pre-studies that productivity growth for many sectors is energy-using, modeling this realtionship causes increasing energy prices (due to environmental policy) to reduce productivity growth rates. In the model, both classes of agents firms (disaggregated to 35 sectors) and households (disaggregated to even 672 representative households) optimize intertemporally. In technical terms this means that two submodels are solved simultanously, one intertemporal one incorporating forward and backward-looking equations to determine the time paths of capital stock and full consumption, and one intratemporal that, using the results of the other submodel, determines prices such that within each time period demand matches supply for all commodity groups.

For the period 1974-1985 Jorgenson and Wilcoxen calculate that U.S. environmental regulation reduced the yearly growth rate by 0.19%, exceeding the estimates of most other studies. The causes for this reduction are split up: the main part being due to mandated investment in pollution control equipment (in the course of new capacity investment or by requiring adaptation of old equipment), followed by motor vehicle regulations. Operating costs due to pollution abatement play only a minor role in the growth slowdown.

1.4.2.3. Multi Country Modeling

The modeling effort most often refered to within OECD countries is the GREEN model. It has been developed within the OECD since 1990 and has been used primarily to compare the effects of various proposals of CO_2 emission curbing policies.[24] The GeneRal Equilibrium ENvironmental model is a multi-sector, multi-region and dynamic CGE model. It was developed on the basis of the WALRAS model (which was constructed in the OECD to evaluate economy-wide effects of agricultural policies), but with a shift in focus towards energy inputs and the intertemporal structure of the model.

The model currently includes twelve regional submodels for the U.S., Japan, EC, other OECD, Central and Eastern Europe, the former Soviet Union, Energy-exporting LDCs, China, India, Dynamic Asian Countries, Brazil and a residual aggregate for the Rest of the World. In the energy markets the model distinguishes three sources of fossil fuels - oil, natural gas and coal - and one source of non-fossil energy - including hydroelectric, nuclear and other carbon-free sources of energy. The advantage of the multicountry model is that all these regions can be linked to each other in detail, most importantly for trade: by bilateral world trade matrices.

The dynamic structure the model involves is currently rather simple. Savings decisions determine the accumulation of productive capital and thereby future economic outcomes; firms investment decisions themselves are not explicitely modeled. Simulation calculations are done over the 1985-2050 period, in steps of five-year intervals. Given the dynamic structure of the model, the evolution over time actually represents a sequence of single-period static equilibria.

The main contribution of GREEN for environmental policy analysis is to combine a large regional coverage with a consistent treatment of world trade flows and energy price distortions. Among the various CO_2 policy simulations it has been used to study, the comparison of the case of

[24] Burniaux et al. (1991, 1992).

OECD or EC acting solely with the case of world-wide action received particular emphasis. While a stabilization of CO_2 emissions in OECD countries at the 1990 level by the year 2000 would entail a 43 percent reduction by 2050 in OECD countries, this only would amount to an 11 per cent reduction in global emisson levels. However, the cost within OECD countries for such policy is suggested to be very small: only a 0.6 per cent reduction of real income. Also the model shows that the carbon leakage effect of unilateral action (via energy market feedback effects) is negligable, though it is higher when only EC countries become policy active.

For world-wide action and using a Toronto-type agreement as the emission-reduction objective, for a uniform carbon tax policy the model suggests that the carbon tax rate would need to rise to 140 US$ per ton of carbon in 2050. Originating from this cost-effective scenario, where most reduction would occur in the coal-based economies (China, India, the former Soviet Union and the CEECs), various forms of redistribution of emission limits can be tested and conclusions can be drawn for inter-country-block financial transfers necessary to induce world-wide policy.

Model results of GREEN, however, covering such a long time horizon, are particularly strongly dependent on the time behavior assumptions used. In particular these are assumptions about the baseline economic growth, the growth of world population and the key model parameters, most importantly the input factor substitution possibilities and energy productivity increases. Most discussion evolves around substitution assumptions. Interfactor and interenergy elasticities of substitution used in GREEN have been based on a survey of the econometric literature. In some aspects there is indication that these historic values underestimate the actual development or at least the potential the future might be characterized by.[25]

[25] Compare Schleicher (1992).

2. The Austrian Environment and Trade Model

Following the overview of the basic ideas and history of CGE modeling we are now to construct the environmental computable general equilibrium model for our policy interest, environment and trade, for the example of the Austrian economy. The model can take benefit from recent experience in European modeling efforts. In particluar its structure and implementation is based on a Swedish model summarized in Bergman (1991), as this model acknowledges the small open economy aspect in a way most appropriate for the analysis of the Austrian context.

2.1. Model Structure

The basic structure of the model shall first be outlined. The subsequent section will then set out the equations in detail.

2.1.1. Production

The main discomfort with the first generation of economy-wide multisectoral environmental policy analysis, based on input-output models, was their restriction to fixed input coefficients. The development of CGE models is primarily grounded on their allowance for endogenous substitution possibilities in inputs.

While this flexibility in input modeling is the objective, we are also asked to keep the functional form as simple as possible, such that the exogenous parameter demand is kept low.[26] The simplest functional form, a Cobb-Douglas production function, is characterized by unit-elasticity of substitution which limits our scope too strongly. The model therefore uses CES (constant elasticity of substitution) production functions, which allow

[26] Compare V.1.3.3.

for the full range of substitution elasticities. As empirical studies show that these elasticities are different between the various factors of production (and groups of them), the structure will be nested to allow for such a differentiation in detail.

As production factors, labor and capital are used as the traditional ones. For the particular environmental emphasis two further factors are introduced, which cover energy aggregates, one for fossil energy and one for electricity.

A survey on the availability of empirical econometric estimates on interfactor and interenergy elasticities of substitution done in the forefield of GREEN, Nicoletti (1990), points out that these elasticities of substitution are best available

- interenergy for electricty and non-electricity
- interfactor for capital and labor (as the least controversial of all elasticites), and for capital and energy. The latter, however, is highly controversial in the empirical findings.

On the basis of this study and on that of Bergman (1991) the following nesting is implemented for the AET-model:

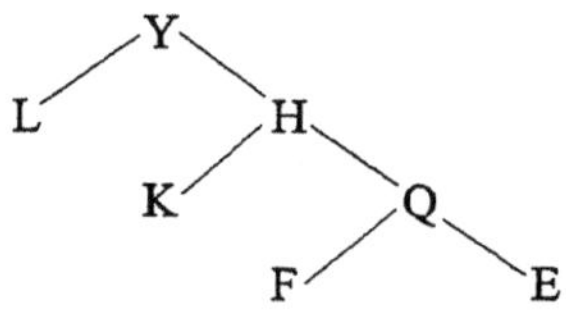

with Y, H and Q the respective level aggregates of the primary factors E (electricity), F (fossil fuels), K (capital) and L (labor).

This hierarchy is in particular superior to one based on a capital-labor bundle, as the *capital*-energy substitutability is usually found different (in the short term far lower) than *labor*-energy substitutability. A capital-labor bundle would imply that energy substitutability would have to be modeled with the same parameter of elasticity with respect to both labor and capital, whereas the structure given above allows for the different substitutability between labor-energy and capital-energy. It also can take advantage of the availability of parameters for labor-capital substitutability, however, interpreting them now for the capital-energy bundle rather than for capital only.

At the very top of the production structure the aggregate of primary factor inputs Y is combined with the intermediate inputs in a Leontieff production function. The reason being, that elasticities of substitution among these intermediate inputs from the other economic sectors are not only not available, but can meaningfully also best be assumed to be given by constant input coefficients, representing the basic (technical) structure of the economy.

The full production structure of the model therefore is given by

(1) $$X_j = \min\left(\frac{Y_j}{A_j}, \frac{X_{ij}}{a_{ij}}\right)$$

(2) $$\begin{aligned} Y_j &= CES(L_j, H_j) \\ H_j &= CES(K_j, Q_j) \\ Q_j &= CES(E_j, F_j) \end{aligned}$$

with i and j indicating the economic sectors, and A_j and a_{ij} representing the Leontieff input-output coefficients.

For sectoral disaggregation the choice follows two criteria, international competition and pollution intensity. Three sectors strongly exposed to the world market and simultanously showing highest pollution intensity (base metals-BASEMET, chemicals-CHEMIC, paper and wood-PAPWOOD) are differentiated from a four-sector aggregation of the remaining sheltered and non-trading sectors, generally less pollution intensive. Of them, the exposed sectors showing some price setting power (textiles, stone and ceramics, and metal manufacturing) are aggregated in the model sector MANUF, the sheltered sectors (agriculture and forestry, food and building and construction) are aggregated in the sector SHELT, services are aggregated in the sector SERV and the public sector is considered seperate as PUBL. Energy production is the final sector, supplying fossil fuels and electricity. In its electricity supply discrimination is made between electricity of current sources and new "substitute" electricity, which partly is produced from fossil fuels itself. The share of caloric production for substitute electricity is a political parameter. For policy simulations in this study the upper bound assumption of sole caloric production is used. Overall fossil fuels imports to the Austrian economy are restricted by the current account.

2.1.2. Trade

A major issue in empirical trade modeling throughout input-output and CGE analysis has been the avoidance of model results of complete specialization in only a few sectors. With the SMOPEC assumption of a world market price taker, a specialization result follows straight from the use of constant returns to scale technology. Given that there are m sectors with tradeables and n factors of production, then if $m >> n$, CRS models will result in complete specialization in n sectors, the output of the other sectors being zero. This simply follows from the rank of the system of equations, as summarized excellently in Taylor (1975), otherwise the system would be overdetermined.

One possibility for avoiding full specialization would be to leave the CRS world. However, any such deviation would imply that the decision on the quantity produced would influence profits. Therefore in this case producer profit optimization decisions would have to include quantity considerations, enlarging the profit maximization behavior equations tremendously. Generally, this is avoided as the price is considered too high.

In CGE modeling there are various ways to avoid such full specialization even when CRS technology is used.

The capital stock per sector could be taken as fixed. The decreasing marginal productivity of labor then would give the necessary upward sloping supply curves. However, for our question, it is exactly the sectoral allocation resulting from environmental policy that we want to explain. By assuming a fixed capital stock this sectoral structure would be treated as fixed.

The most broadly used approach is to base the model on the so called Armington-assumption.[27] According to it the goods sold within each sector domestically are regarded as composite goods, made up by a combination of domestically produced and imported goods of this category. The mix depends on the relative price of the two.

In graphic terms:

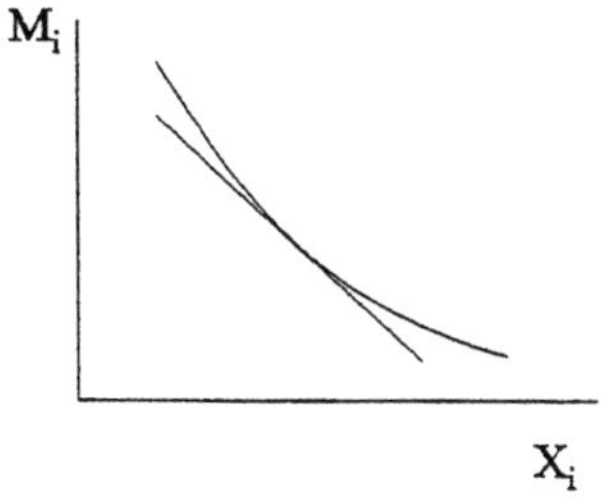

with M_i representing the imports of goods category i and X_i domestic supply originating from domestic production.

[27] Originally put forward in Armington (1969).

The export side can be modeled equivalently. Production within a country is assumed to be different according to whether it is subsequently sold domestically or exported. The share of exports therein again depends on the relative price that is observed on the world market versus that of domestic production. However, in the export case this assumption does not have an actual empirical basis. Domestic goods sold on the domestic market will in most cases not really differ from those sold to the world market, therefore, empirically, the current share of exports is simply assumed to represent a different good.

Again, the price ratio determines the location on the production possibility frontier:

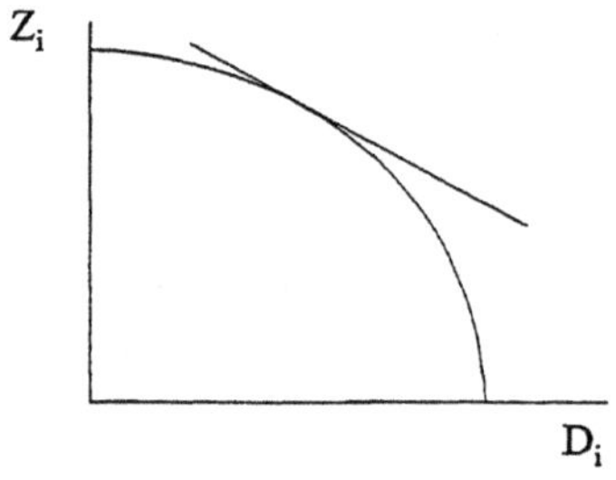

with Z_i representing the exports of goods of category i and D_i domestic production for the domestic market of sector i.

A third possibility to prevent complete specialization would be to reduce the number of tradeables sectors (m) to below the number of domestic factors (n). However, sectoral disaggregation data is empirically generally better available than data for a detailed *factor* modeling on a very disaggregated level.

In the AET model a combination of the latter two strategies is chosen. It is considered useful to explicitely model the strongly exposed sectors as such, but their number is kept to only three. The remaining sectors (excluding energy production, which is covered below) are modeled according to the Armington assumption. For simplicity it is only net exports that are considered, their amount being dependent on the ratio between the world and domestic price levels and on an export market growth parameter.

Net exports Z_i in the price-setting-power sectors are given by

$$(3) \quad Z_i = Z_i^0 \left(\frac{P_i}{P_i^W}\right)^{\varepsilon_i} e^{\gamma . t}$$

with ε_i being the price elasticity of export demand and γ.t allowing the modeling of growth in the export market. P_i is the producer price in sector i, P_i^W the world market price in this sector.

In the strongly exposed sectors the sectoral foreign balance is a residuum such that the gap between domestic supply and domestic demand is filled (by exports or imports, respectively).

The strongly exposed sectors are international price-takers:

$$(4) \quad P_i^D = P_i^W = (1 + \tau_i) P_i$$

where P_i^D is the domestic consumer price level and P_i is the producer price net of indirect taxes and subsidies, τ_i is a sectoral ad valorem tax rate.

For the sheltered sectors the Armington assumption implies some price setting power. The price level in these sectors therefore is independent of the world market price level:

$$(5) \quad P_i^D = (1 + \tau_i) P_i .$$

As the empirical analysis will show, such a foreign trade modeling - three sectors with perfect competition, the remaining sectors with some price setting power (Armington assumption), in the presence of three domestic primary input factors - does not force the model to specialization. However, it by no means guarantees that specialization will not occur.

Therefore, for the exposed sectors the model includes a further characteristic. Exposed sectors are dependent on the world market price. If the world market price (or its expectation) in one of these sectors falls below costs (or their expectations, respectively), obviously no further investment will take place, but the "old" capital stock available might nevertheless be used for production, and will be to some extent. A modeling of this behavior can avoid bang-bang results of extreme switches in sectoral production.

The AET model distinguishes for the exposed sectors between "old" production units (those available already at the base period) and new production capital arising from new investment since the base period.

The degree of utilization of old production units is dependent on the rent on this capital:

$$(6) \quad \begin{aligned} X_i^{OLD} &= R_i^{\varepsilon_s} Cap_i \\ P_i^W &= MC_i^{OLD} + R_i Cap_i \end{aligned}$$

with X_i^{OLD} representing the quantity of production in old production units, R_i the rent in these units, which is determined by the gap between the remaining cost factors and the world market price, MC_i^{OLD} standing for the marginal costs excluding capital cost, Cap for the production capacity available in this sector and ε_S for the supply elasticity of old capital.

2.1.3. Environment

2.1.3.1. Emissions

For the environmental focus of the AET model air pollution is chosen for a threefold reason. First, data availability in this area is given, better than in most other areas. Second, for most components the location of emission release is not as important as in other fields (e.g. water pollution). Finally, air pollution is among the issues in intense political discussion, which supplies environmental quality objective levels for policy analysis.

For one component of air pollution, CO_2 emissions, the place of release is irrelevant even on the international level. Therefore its contribution to the greenhouse effect can serve as the best example available to study unilateral environmental policy action for the resolution (or diminution) of a truly global environmental problem. Fully coordinated action is in the interest of most countries, but nevertheless they seek different policy stringency levels. CO_2 policy is chosen as the main modeling focus in order to analyze the quantitive effects environmental policy has in an open economy, comparing various ways of its implementation. The model also covers air pollution in SO_2 and NO_x, but primarily for the quantification of CO_2 policy accompanying benefits rather than for direct reduction policy in these pollutants, where the Austrian emission levels of SO_2 in particular have been reduced substantially already within the last decade.

CO_2 emissions are directly related to fuel use, irrespective of the process of production (or combustion) used and without any end-of-pipe abatement option. Emissions are therefore generated in the model via emission coefficients that are related to sectoral fuel use. Emission coefficients differ across production sectors and the household sector, as each of them employs a different mix within fossil fuels. For the medium term these mixes are assumed constant.

2.1.3.2. Environmental Policy

The model is used for comparative static analysis. After model calibration to the data of the year 1990 it is run in a base case scenario for the year 2005 assuming no further environmental policy than currently implemented in Austria (and reflected in the coefficients of the model). The economic and emission data that this base case gives is used as a reference for the policy scenarios; each a comparative static analysis.

For the actually available multitude of policy instruments, two are selected, representative for any - economically efficient - policy implemeted: tradeable emission permits and emission taxes.

The permit price only becomes positive when the (policy) emission limit becomes binding. The price rises to a level that ensures meeting the emission objective.

Permit costs and emission taxes are causally related to fuel use. Actually, they can be seen as fuel factor price components and are modeled as such. Thereby, environmental policy changes factor prices and impacts producer and consumer decisions, and in particular gives rise to factor substitution.

The fuel price in each sector is denoted by

(7) $$P_i^F = P^F + (\pi + \tau_i^e) emk_i$$

with P^F giving the base price of fuels (import price plus indirect taxes), π denoting the permits price, τ_i^e the environmental tax rate on CO_2 emissions in sector i and emk_i representing the sectoral emission coefficient.

2.1.3.3. The Energy Sector

The energy sector supplies the two energy aggregates, fossil fuels and electricity. Fuels originate in a constant yearly amount from within Austria, but in their majority are imported. Fuel demand of production, of private consumption and for use in substitute electricity production above domestic supply therefore affect the current account. For the medium term Austria is not allowed to run into excessive current account deficits or surpluses, the model is closed by fixing the current account balance at its 1990 (roughly balanced) level. Additional fuel imports therefore have to be matched by improvements in the remaining products trade balance.

Electricity supply is assumed to be given at the 1990 supply level. Only additional electricity supply is explicitely modeled. The production of this substitute electricity requires both fuel and capital inputs. The fuel input ratio (and thereby the emission impact) is basically a political decision on the mix in the kind of additional supply chosen, hydroelectric power plants, thermal power plants fueld by gas, oil or coal, or solar technology. For the policy scenarios the environmental impact upper bound assumption is used of solely thermal production. For derivation of the emission coefficient, the 1985-1990 average emissions originating from Austrian thermal power plants are used.

Total electricity supply is given by

(8) $E = E^{1990} + X_E$

with X_E denoting the production of substitute electricity. For this, production capital demand is given by

(9) $k_E * X_E$

and fuel demand for substitute electricity production by

(10) $a_E * X_E$

with k_E and a_E denoting the respective input coefficients.

Substitute electricity is produced only when the price for electricity covers its cost of production.

2.2. Formal Description

2.2.1. Costs

The model is specified directly in cost duals. As the technology is specified to show constant returns to scale, the marginal and average cost in sector j is denoted by

$$(11) \quad MC_j = P_{Yj} A_j e^{-\lambda t} + \sum_i P_i^D a_{ij} + b_j$$

with P_{Yj} denoting the price index of the primary factor production aggregate Y as described in section V.2.1.1., λ_j denoting yearly productivity index growth and b_j the indirect tax per unit of sector j output.

To derive the price index P_{Yj} the nested production structure has to be employed, deriving the price indices for the aggregate of each level.

Exemplifying, we shall derive the price index for the lowest level in detail.

Given the CES production function

$$(12) \quad Q_j = (\delta_{Qj} E^{\frac{\sigma_{Qj}-1}{\sigma_{Qj}}} + (1-\delta_{Qj}) F^{\frac{\sigma_{Qj}-1}{\sigma_{Qj}}})^{\frac{\sigma_{Qj}}{\sigma_{Qj}-1}}$$

where σ_{Qj} denotes the elasticity of substitution between electricity and fuels in the production of composite energy in sector j and δ_{Qj} is a distribution parameter, and the output price equation for Q (for matters of notational simplicity we write just P for P_Q and also supress elasticity level and sectoral indices from now on)

$$(13)\quad P = P_E \frac{E}{Q} + P_F \frac{F}{Q}$$

we can use the optimality conditions implied by producer profit maximizing behavior of the price ratio equalizing the marginal factor productivities

$$(14)\quad \frac{P_E}{P} = \delta (\frac{Q}{E})^{\frac{1}{\sigma}}$$

and

$$(15)\quad \frac{P^F}{P} = (1-\delta)(\frac{Q}{F})^{\frac{1}{\sigma}},$$

transform them to

$$(14')\quad (\frac{P_E}{P})^{\sigma} = \delta^{\sigma} \frac{Q}{E} \qquad \text{which gives} \quad \frac{E}{Q} = \delta^{\sigma} P_E^{-\sigma} P^{\sigma} \qquad \text{and}$$

$$(15')\quad (\frac{P_F}{P})^{\sigma} = \delta^{\sigma} \frac{Q}{F} \qquad \text{which gives} \quad \frac{F}{Q} = \delta^{\sigma} P_F^{-\sigma} P^{\sigma} \qquad ,$$

such that we can substitute (14´) and (15´) into (13), which results in

$$(16)\quad P = \delta^{\sigma} P_E^{1-\sigma} P^{\sigma} + (1-\delta)^{\sigma} P_F^{(1-\sigma)} P^{\sigma}$$

and gives the requested price index as

$$(17)\quad P = (\delta^{\sigma} P_E^{(1-\sigma)} + (1-\delta)^{\sigma} P_F^{(1-\sigma)})^{\frac{1}{1-\sigma}} .$$

Equivalently the price index for the next level aggregates are given by

$$(18)\quad P_{Hj} = (\delta_{Hj}{}^{\sigma_{Hj}} P_K{}^{(1-\sigma_{Hj})} + (1-\delta_{Hj})^{\sigma_{Hj}} P_Q{}^{(1-\sigma_{Hj})})^{\frac{1}{1-\sigma_{Hj}}} \text{ and}$$

$$(19)\quad P_{Yj} = (\delta_{Yj}{}^{\sigma_{Yj}} P_L{}^{(1-\sigma_{Yj})} + (1-\delta_{Yj})^{\sigma_{Yj}} P_H{}^{(1-\sigma_{Yj})})^{\frac{1}{1-\sigma_{Yj}}} \quad .$$

2.2.2. Demand

The primary focus of the model is its production side to determine competitive effects. Therefore intermediate demand is determined in respective detail according to the technology assumptions given in the input-output table. For final demand in the domestic market, a modeling approach of a simple functional form is chosen. As in Bergman (1991) also in the AET model final demand is given by a linear expenditure system, which is due to consumer utility being assumed of the Cobb-Douglas form. Final demand is a composite of private consumption demand, public demand and investment demand.

Domestic final demand in each sectoral and energy category is given by

$$(20)\quad D_i = \overline{D_i} + \frac{\beta_i}{P_i^D}(I - \sum_i P_i^D \overline{D_i}) \text{ for i=BASEMET, CHEMIC,}$$

PAPWOOD, MANUF, SHELT,
SERV, PUBL, Fuels, Electricity

with $\overline{D_i}$ denoting the exogenous demand of each goods category, β_i the marginal expenditure share for goods category i and I the total of disposable income for domestic end use net of savings.

2.2.3. Producer Behavior

In the strongly exposed sectors, producers have to adjust their production quantities to the given world market prices. In the form of the Kuhn-Tucker conditions

$$(21)\quad \begin{aligned} &P_i - MC_i \leq 0 \\ &(P_i - MC_i)X_i = 0 \\ &X_i \geq 0 \end{aligned}$$

indicating that either the price equals marginal costs, or alternatively, when $P < MC$, output is zero.

In the sheltered and non-trading sectors, the domestic price level is determined by production costs.

$$(22)\quad P_i = MC_i$$

Similarly as in the exposed sectors, in substitute electricity production, the output level is dependent on the price of electricity, such that the optimality conditions are met

$$(23)\quad \begin{aligned} &P_E - MC_E \leq 0 \\ &(P_E - MC_E)X_E = 0 \\ &X_E \geq 0 \end{aligned}$$

2.2.4. Permits Market

The actual model policy parameter "upper limit of emissions" can be interpretetd as a correspondingly high amount of emission permits sold. The price of the emission permits is determined by the market equilibrium conditions in the permits market

$$Em - EmLIM \leq 0$$
$$(24) \quad \pi_e(Em - EmLIM) = 0$$
$$\pi_e \geq 0$$

They ensure that the emission limit (EmLIM) is not exceeded, and that the permit´s price π_e is only positive when the limit is binding.

2.2.5. GDP

Gross domestic product is defined as the sum of all primary factor incomes (labor, capital, electricity, domestic fuel production), indirect taxes and environmental revenues (environmental charges and permit sale income).

2.3. Data Basis

2.3.1. Social Accounting Matrix

The availability of disaggregated official economic data in Austria is characterized by a level of especially high detail. Therefore it is not supplied on a yearly basis, but for selected base years roughly in a seven year periodicity. Currently, however, for various circumstances, the latest official data available is that of 1976.

Yet at the Austrian Institute of Economic Research, Fritz Breuss has imputed a 19 sector SAM for the base year of 1990, which he kindly offered to form the data basis for the AET model.

The SAM for the AET model was constructed on this data basis, the structure of which is given in Breuss and Tesche (1991). The adjustments made from the 19-sector SAM were the following.

Data was aggregated into a seven sector-specification, using as criterion the degree of competitiveness as explained above and the quantitive export positions as given in table A.3. Table A.2 denotes the chosen aggregation.

The SAM was extended for rows and columns for the factors fuels and electricity. The sum of their inputs was substracted from the intermediate input from the energy covering sector, SERV. This sector, SERV, however, continues to supply the domestic mining of fossil fuels and the amount of electricity it suppplied in the year 1990, which are both modeled as constant, exogenous demand for the output of the sector SERV.

For the import of fuels and the final demand of fuels and electricity, these factors are secondly also introduced in both the activities and commodities category.

2.3.2. Energy Expenses

Data on energy expenses is based on ÖSTAT (1992)[28], which gives energy expenses on a 43 sector disaggregation. Energy expenses (net of transformation energy) is first aggregated into the standard 19 sector specification for each category of energy, as given in table A.4. The latest data available, however, refers to 1988. Currently a methodological discussion is further delaying more recent data. To transform the energy expense data to 1990 levels, a distinction was made between fuels and electricity. For fuels the real change was based on the change in CO_2 emissions between 1988 and 1990, made available by UBA (1992)[29] on a sectorally somewhat detailed basis. The assumptions used are given in table A.5. Real increase in electricity demand was based on the

---

[28] Monetäre Aufwendungen für den energetischen Endverbrauch im Jahr 1988, ÖSTAT (1992b) : 1027-1035.

[29] CO2-Emissionsentwicklung und Prognose für Österreich, UBA (1992): 6.

development of total electricity supply, given in ÖSTAT (1990, 1992a)[30], assuming equal increase across sectors.

For both kinds of energy the nominal change then was derived on the basis of the energy price development supplied by ÖSTAT (1990,1991)[31]. Finally, energy expense data is aggregated to the seven production sectors of the AET model and private demand, as given in table A.6.

2.3.3. Energy Supply

Electricity supply, split according to means of production, is given in table A.7, based on ÖSTAT (1990,1991,1992a). As hydroelectric supply was exceptionally low in the base year 1990, for the comparative static analysis, a four year average of 1988-1991 of hydroelectric supply is used instead.

The energy balance distinguishing between domestic and imported fuels for the year 1990 is given in table A.8 in physical units. Using the average fuel price of the AET model derived from energy demand in GJ of industries and their respective expenses, data is transformed to the monetary 1990 flow data for the AET-SAM.

2.3.4. Emissions

On the basis of UBA (1992) and internal emission data of the Austrian Institute of Economic Research, the sectorally disaggregated emissions in CO_2, SO_2 and NO_x have been calculated.

---

[30] Energieversorgung Österreich, Jahreshefte 1989, 1991, Tab. Gesamte Elektrizitätsversorgung in Österreich.

[31] op. cit., Tab. 7.3. Implizite Energieeinstandpreise der Industriebetriebe.

2.3.5. Time Behavior Parameters

2.3.5.1. Productivity Changes

To give information on the likely sectoral structure of productivity changes, those of past experience have been surveyed.

First, labor productivity changes are calculated for the AET disaggregation on the basis of Lager (1993), stated in Table A.9. In detail he finds that the development of labor productivity changes over time can best be characterized by a function of logistic behavior, indicating lower values for the period of analysis in our study. He also finds capital productivity to be roughly constant over time.

Sectoral energy productivity changes have been calculated on the basis of the nominal energy expenses per unit of output supplied by ÖSTAT (1976, 1992c) disaggregated to 43 sectors, and the BIP-deflator. Energy productivity changes for the period 1974-1989 at the 19 sector level are given in table A.10.

Based on the combination of these factor productivity changes and in consideration of the subsequently described assumptions on supply growth in primary factors, the following sectoral overall yearly productivity changes are implemented in the AET model.

Tab. 5.1. Productivity Changes AET-Model

[yearly % averages]

sector		
[1]	Basemet	0,6
[2]	Chemic	0,2
[3]	Papwood	0,0
[4]	Manuf	1,4
[5]	Shelt	0,9
[6]	Serv	1,1
[7]	Publ	0,3

2.3.5.2. Factor Growth

The change in supply in energy factors is modeled endogenously as described above in the section model structure.

Factor growth in labor is assumed to continue at the 1966-1992 average rate of 0,95% per year.[32] Factor growth in capital service supply is assumed at 1,85% per year.[33]

2.3.5.3. Elasticities of Substitution

Nicoletti (1990) in his survey on interfactor and interenergy elasticities of substitution distinguishes empirical estimates available according to the geographic area they refer to. For the group of the EFTA countries the literature suggests elasticities in the following range.

Tab. 5.2. Elasticities of Substitution, EFTA-Countries
(survey on econometric studies; Nicoletti, 1990)

Interfactor:	
Labor - Capital	0,5 - 0,7
Capital - Energy	0,4 - 0,8
Interenergy:	
Electricity - Non-Electricity	0,9 - 1,5

For the elasticities of the AET model generally the mean values of these ranges are used. Only for capital substitutability a lower value is used. The reason being that the econometric interenergy elasticity of substitution estimates are usually based on the assumption that capital and energy are weakly seperable. Basically, this rests on a context where firms first choose a cost-minimizing energy-mix and subsequently choose the optimal capital-energy bundle.

[32] Derived on the basis of ÖSTAT (1993), Tab. 15.2. Beschäftigung und Arbeitsmarkt.

[33] The 1964-1992 average yearly growth rate has been higher, but growth rates are declining since the early seventies.

The elasticities used for the base run of the AET model are given in table 5.3.

Tab. 5.3. Elasticities of Substitution AET-Model

Labor - (Capital, Energy)	0,60
Capital - Energy	0,45
Electricity - Fuels	1,20

2.4. Implementation

There are currently two main software environments used by the international scientific community to implement CGE-models. The two environments imply different degrees of both restriction on the model structure and explicit specification demand.

The environment supplying quicker specification is MPS/GE, developed by Thomas Rutherford at the University of Western Ontario[34] . For the General Equilibrium application it was expanded in particular in cooperation with Glenn Harrison; the approach is described in Rutherford (1988). The very straightforwardness of the user-interface draws on a restriction on the model structure to require production functions to be of the nested CES-form. Such the user practically only specifies his choice of aggregate composition and is asked to enter the values of elasticity of substitution. While MPS/GE requires a production structure that is indeed widely used in modeling, it nevertheless, also in that cases, is restrictive on modeling some special problem features, such as model complexity requiring different solution algorithms, or in the specification of boundary conditions.

The much more flexible environment, but therefore somewhat more demanding, is the General Algebraic Modeling System language (GAMS).

[34] Currently: University of Colorado.

It was developed primarily at the World Bank based on the empirical modeling experience at this institution. A detailed description is supplied by Brooke et al. (1988). GAMS merges concepts of relational database theory and mathematical programming. The baseline objective is to seperate model representation and solution algorithms, such that various optimization procedures can be applied without changing model representation. Currently GAMS covers a range of solvers for linear, non-linear and mixed integer optimizations. In GAMS the optimization problem is expressed independently of the explicit data used, which allows for an increase in model size without an increase in the complexity of representation. The relational data model also allows for automated allocation of computer resources, such that the user is relieved from these concerns. The seperation of model representation and solution algorithms eases the portability of models considerably. All the model information is contained in a relatively small model code file.

For the reasons of modeling flexibility and easiness in international exchange, but also grounded in the implementation of the Swedish model kindly supplied by Lars Bergman to form the basis of the current research, the AET-model is implemented in the GAMS language. The most recent version 2.25 was used, the main improvement of which compared to earlier versions is in its larger options for programming interfaces with other application software. As solver primarily the non-linear solver GAMS/CONOPT was applied, as described in Drud (1992). CONOPT is a FORTRAN-based generalized reduced gradient (GRG) algorithm that was developed specifically for models that are characterized by large size and higher non-linearity.

3. Policy Simulations-The Effects of Unilateral Policy

3.1. Base Case

Given the economic, energy and environmental data as described above, the model is calibrated for the year 1990. Calibration gives the final set of missing parameters, namely the individual primary factor shares δ_i in the production functions of each sector.

For policy analysis a comparative static approach is chosen. First the base case for the year 2005 - as CGE results are sensible best for medium term investigation - is solved as a reference scenario. In this base case there is no environmental concern, i.e. emissions are not limited exogenously.

Our main interest is in (a) the development of the structure of the economy, (b) the development of relative factor prices, and (c) the development of demand for the environmentally most relevant factors, fuels and electricity. The latter is best seen in private consumption of these factors, fuels and electricity, as the model involves a linear expenditure system. Table 5.4 states the developments of these selected variables for the base case.

For convenience, absolute changes ocurring in this fifteen year time period are expressed in average yearly growth rates. Overall real GNP growth is at 2%. Sectorally we observe strong differentiation, however. Our first interest is in the exposed sectors. The particular development within this subgroup is strongly dependent on the combination of world market price changes and sectoral productivity growth rates. For the base case scenario data base of currently available predictions, results indicate a decline of the sectors base metals and paper and wood, whereas there is growth in the chemicals sector.

Tab. 5.4. Base Case Results
selected economic variables

	1990	2005	yearly change [%]
real GNP	1848,2	2483,6	2,0
electricity consumption	18,0	23,9	1,9
fuel consumption	46,1	60,0	1,8
Output in			
BASEMET	58,5	42,8	-2,1
CHEMIC	121,4	215,8	3,9
PAPWOOD	208,7	167,9	-1,4
MANUF	502,3	718,4	2,4
SHELT	611,4	857,7	2,3
SERV	1416,5	2098,4	2,7
PUBL	404,8	538,7	1,9
Price index of			
Capital	1,00	0,97	-0,2
Labor	1,00	1,20	1,2
Electricity	1,00	1,06	0,4
Emissions			
CO2 [mio. t]	59,55	68,72	1,0

For the sheltered and non-trading sectors, model results indicate growth above or approximately at the overall growth rate, between 1.9% in the public sector and 2.65% in the services sector.

The private demand in energy increases somewhat below the growth rate of the economy, as relative prices of energy slightly increase, the electricity price index increasing by 0.4% per year. Capital gets relatively more abundant, the capital price index decreases 0.2% per year. Only the labor price changes more strongly, indicating relative shortage.

CO_2 emissions increase from 59.55 mio. t in 1990 to 68.72 mio. t in 2005. This model result corresponds closely to the 2005 prediction of UBA (1992) at 68.5 mio. t. It implies an average yearly growth by 1.0%.

3.2. Environmental Policy

Our interest is in the activity level effects, overall and sectoral, that environmental policy provokes if undertaken unilaterally in the small open economy of Austria. As stringency level a stabilization of CO_2 emissions at the 1990 level is chosen. Such a proposal is being promoted, for example, by some countries within the EC, but agreement uppon coordinated action still appears to be a long way off.[35]

3.2.1. Unilateral, Sectorally Uniform Environmental Policy

When CO_2 emissions are stabilized this corresponds to a reduction compared to the 2005 base case of about 13%. As the results summarized in table 5.5. indicate, the impact such a reduction has on GNP growth is hardly observable. There are, however, sectoral shifts. For the trade perspective of environmental policy, the exposed sectors are of highest interest. While for two of them the chosen CO_2 policy, similar as for the overall economy, hardly influences activity levels, for one sector, base metals, environmental policy cuts output in half.

Tab. 5.5. Effects of Unilateral CO2 Policy
values for 2005

	base case {1}	policy case {2}	{2}:{1}
real GDP	2483,6	2476,3	0,997
electricity consumption	23,9	22,7	0,950
fuel consumption	60,0	58,5	0,975
Output in			
BASEMET	42,8	19,7	0,460
CHEMIC	215,8	226,3	1,049
PAPWOOD	167,9	168,9	1,006
MANUF	718,4	714,2	0,994
SHELT	857,7	857,6	1,000
SERV	2098,4	2107,5	1,004
PUBL	538,7	540,7	1,004
Price index of			
Capital	0,97	0,96	0,990
Labor	1,20	1,18	0,983
Electricity	1,06	1,15	1,085

Environmental policy obviously also reduces private consumption of both fuels and electricity. Relative factor prices shift towards a further increase of electricity cost and a correspponding slight decrease of the relative prices of both labor and capital.

---

35 At the EC environmental ministerial council Oct. 5, 1993, for example, the German environmental minister Klaus Töpfer affirmatively launched a corresponding proposal. *Salzburger Nachrichten* Oct. 6, p. 6.

The model in this run also supplies the marginal cost of abatement for CO_2 emission stabilization in 2005 at 0,26 AS/kg CO_2.[36] Hofer (1993)[37] surveys total (not marginal) reduction costs per unit of CO_2 for the full range of available technologies in detail, their range being from 0,24 AS/kg to 63,19 AS/kg. Considering the life-span of these investments the AET model result indicates that for the policy case chosen only the currently cheaper abatement technologies are necessary and will pay. They include switching from individual home heating systems to district heating or biogas shared heating systems. They do not include solar or photovoltaic technology, which currently have a CO_2 reduction cost of 29 and 22 AS/kg respectively.

3.2.2. Unilateral, Sectorally Differentiated Environmental Policy

From the potentially strong effect environmental policy can have on exposed sectors a policy framing demand might arise to mitigate these effects. A major proposal is to exempt such sectors from environmental policy.

Environmental policy, however, is connected with a range of indirect effects throughout the economy. If exposed sectors (which are often also the highest pollution intensive sectors) are exempted, in order to reach the same reduction objective, policy has to be quite a bit stricter in other sectors. The question then is whether indirect effects of policy in these sectors on the exempted sectors - via price changes of intermediate and primary factor inputs - would be so strong that the exemption would not effectively mitigate the international competitive disadvantage.

When the tax, as commonly proposed, focuses strongly on private consumption and is set for this group at 1,12 AS/kg, model results indicate that for the regulated production sectors the environmental tax

---

36 1990 AS. This number corresponds to 11,3 US$/bbl. oil (using an exchange rate of 11 AS/US$), a level that is discussed and partly in effect as CO_2 tax in Europe. Poterba (1991), p. 74, reports carbon tax rates on gasoline and fuels in 1990 for Sweden at 16 $/bbl, for Finland at 11,5 $/bbl and for the Netherlands at 2,7 $/bbl.

37 Hofer (1993), pp. 42-50.

needs to be raised from 0,26 of the uniform policy case to 0,51 AS in order to meet the CO_2 emission stabilization objective for the overall economy.

The structural and relative price effects such a differentiated policy brings about in the AET model are presented in table 5.6. First, results indicate that in spite of the distorted environmental policy, stabilization of emissions again can be reached with practically unchanged growth in the overall activity level. Second, results reveal that activity declines in exposed sectors indeed can be largely avoided by sectoral policy differentiation. Thus the indirect effects on exposed sectors via intermediate and primary factor markets are quantitfied to only slightly impact the international competitive position.

Tab. 5.6. Effects of Unilateral CO2 Policy, Sectorally Differentiated
values for 2005

	base case {1}	diff. policy {2}	{2}:{1}
real GDP	2483,6	2483,8	1,000
electricity consumption	23,9	21,1	0,883
fuel consumption	60,0	52,4	0,873
Output in			
BASEMET	42,8	40,6	0,949
CHEMIC	215,8	193,5	0,897
PAPWOOD	167,9	168,1	1,001
MANUF	718,4	716,4	0,997
SHELT	857,7	857,3	1,000
SERV	2098,4	2100,2	1,001
PUBL	538,7	540,3	1,003
Price index of			
Capital	0,97	0,95	0,979
Labor	1,20	1,19	0,992
Electricity	1,06	1,31	1,236

The cost of the - when pursued in the long run, economic inefficient, because distorting - policy is a substantial further increase in energy prices. Fuel price increases differ across sectors depending on initial sectoral fuel prices and fuel mix. The effects can be better compared at the electricity price development. The electricity price now increases by 31%, and again causes both other primary factor price indices to decline to allow for substitution towards these factors. Compared to the uniform policy case there is a slightly stronger substitution towards capital, because less capital is needed in the production of substitute electricity.

3.3. Conclusions

Policy simulation within the AET model has supplied the marginal cost of abatement for CO_2 stabilization to be at 0,26 AS/kg. Comparing the technical CO_2 literature (e.g. Hofer 1993), this tells which of the currently available technologies will pay and will be necessary in such a reduction scenario.

Simulation results also indicated that environmental policy of this stringency can take place at practically unchanged overall GNP growth. Sectorally, however, results diverge.

When unilateral reduction policy is implemented uniformly across the economy, exposed sectors may be affected by serious output declines due to international competitive effects. However, for mitigation of these effects exposed sectors can be exempted from environmental policy. Simulation results in testing this case identify indirect impact on the exposed sectors which is still relevant as being small, so that output decline can indeed be effectively avoided. Further, even in spite of an in this case highly distorted environmental policy, CO_2 stabilization can still be reached at an unchanged GNP growth rate.

In table 5.7. quantitative results of the two policy cases are compared directly. They indicate that such policy differentiation has a much larger effect in the energy sector than the implementation of reduction per se as compared to the base case. The electricity price index increases by 31% versus 15% in the uniform case. Nevertheless, substitute electricity production decreases more, as do fuel imports. Corresponding to the price increases, private energy consumption decreases for both electricity and fuels far more than the decrease triggered by uniform policy.

These results indicate that policy differentiation can very successfully mitigate competitive effects, but that it involves readiness for technology switches in the economy of an order of magnitude higher than implied by just the reduction objective itself.

Tab. 5.7. Effects of Policy Differentiation
values for 2005

	base case	uniform policy	diff. policy
real GDP	2483,6	2476,3	2483,8
electricity consumption	23,9	22,7	21,1
fuel consumption	60,0	58,5	52,4
Output in			
BASEMET	42,8	19,7	40,6
CHEMIC	215,8	226,3	193,5
PAPWOOD	167,9	168,9	168,1
MANUF	718,4	714,2	716,4
SHELT	857,7	857,6	857,3
SERV	2098,4	2107,5	2100,2
PUBL	538,7	540,7	540,3
Price index of			
Capital	0,97	0,96	0,95
Labor	1,20	1,18	1,19
Electricity	1,06	1,15	1,31
Fuels import	74,8	70,4	63,8
Substitute electricity	11,1	8,1	5,1

3.4. Benefits

CO_2 emission reduction policy causes switches in primary factor input. These switches also impact the development of emissions of other pollutants. In particular the decrease in fuel demand causes a range of other pollutant´s emission levels to fall. Aside from mitigating the greenhous effect, CO_2 policy therefore involves further environmental benefits that can be quantified.

The AET model covers the development of SO_2 and NO_x emissions.[38] Stabilization of CO_2 emission at the 1990 level for the year 2005 results in a simultanous reduction (compared to the base case) of SO_2 emissions by 6% and NO_x emissions by 5% for the undifferentiated policy case. For the differentiated policy case reduction levels double, as they involve a more substantial fuel consumption decrease. Reductions in the differentiated case amount to 12% for both SO_2 and NO_x emissions.

This physical emission reduction quantification in principle allows for a monetarization of the accompanying benefits. However, especially for NO_x emissions, their (damaging) effect depends strongly on the location in which they arise, with much stronger effects in generally already heavily polluted densely populated areas. The Austrian Ministry of the Environment is currently in the process of concluding initial results of the development of a land register map to cover air pollution emissions and immissions. This data base can substantially improve the appropriateness of benefit monetarization. The quantification therefore is not to be done without this data shortly available.

However, for this point in time there are indications in the international literature on the approximate range these benefits amount to. Brendemoen and Vennemo (1992) study the effects of CO_2 policy on the development of nine air pollutants in the Norwegian economy.[39] For a somewhat stricter "climate convention scenario" (CO_2 emission stabilization at the 1987 level by the year 2000 and increases of 0,6% thereafter), they determine a broad range of simultanous local benefits. These benefits include health benefits due to emission reduction, but also reduction in noise and traffic accidents triggered by an increase in energy prices. In their study such quantifiable benefits outweigh 80% of the GDP reduction (growth is reduced by a yearly 0,1%) that is triggered by CO_2 policy.

---

[38] In the current version NO_x and SO_x emissions are calculated simply on the basis of constant (1991 based) fuel emission coefficients.

[39] Compare the detailed survey of their study in section V.1.4.2.1.

3.5. Evaluation of the CGE Approach

The idea of computable general equilibrium modeling is to develop a consistent framework that fully covers all indirect effects policy exerts in an economy. Such effects are of particular relevance for a far reaching environmental policy such as the discussed introduction of carbon emission taxes. CGE modeling succeeds in providing detailed information on the structural shifts such policy causes. For the trade and environment question at hand in this study, it is the different effects on exposed sectors versus sheltered and non-trading sectors that can be effectively analyzed.

However, the limits of the CGE modeling approach must also be acknowledged. Most importantly, a static CGE model is not to be used for forecasts on the time development of the overall activity level. Its results are based on the employment of the input factors given; in comparative static analysis they are given exogenously for the future point in time. Instead, time series development has to be studied in an econometric framework and the exogenous CGE framework data must be consistent with this data. The AET model draws on such predictions with respect to factor supply and factor productivity growth, and thereby the resulting real GNP growth of 2% for the base case is consistent with usual forecasts.

For the case of environmental policy, of particular relevance in this respect are likely influences this policy exerts on the formation of capital, both as to its amount and its kind. The latter is standing for the kind of technological progress and innovation that determines productivity. There are initial dynamic CGE models that acknowledge this fact (Hazilla and Kopp (1990), Jorgenson and Wilcoxen (1990)). However, each of them has to remain restricted to a very simple causal link between environmental policy and capital formation, so that the model remains solvable. Hazilla and Kopp, for example, use savings driven investment. As environmental regulation lowers the relative price of leisure it thereby reduces savings, and consequently also investment. Jorgenson and

Wilcoxen in their study model productivity growth as being energy demanding. Environmental policy raises energy prices and therefore productivity growth is reduced. As these models need to concentrate on only one link the question remains whether they really succeed in choosing the most important one, given that there is a truly dominating one at all. While full endogenization of technological progress is appealing, due to the given limitations, in the AET model, technological progress is modeled differently. In the sectors of highest pollution intensity, the model distinguishes between "old" capital (i.e. capital present at the base year 1990), and "new" capital, originating from subsequent investment. Productivity parameters change over time only for the new capital, representing technological progress. While the parameters themselves in this modeling have to be determined exogenously, the choice of speed of transition to this new capital is endogenous.

Progress in full endogenous modeling appears to be closer ahead in a sub-area, that of environmental protection industry development. At the U.S. EPA Nestor and Pasurka have implemented a preliminary CGE version for Germany,[40] and are currently improving the underlying input-output table.[41]

A second particular limitation with respect to the environment and trade question regards the comparison of unilateral versus coordinated environmental action. As this involves inter-country feedback mechanisms, for an appropriate answer individual country behavior would need to be modeled explicitely, thus requiring a multi-country CGE framework. Such modeling, while very rewarding, however, also demands very high modeling effort. Therefore the two currently existing multicountry environmental CGE models have been constructed and are maintained in a scientist group effort.

---

[40] Nestor and Pasurka (1992).

[41] Nestor and Pasurka (1993b).

The first environmental CGE on the Austrian economy therefore has been constructed as a single country model at this point in time. This framework is the appropriate one for discussing *intra*-country policy shaping, such as the crucial question of the environmental and competitive effects of policy that exempts exposed, but usually simultanously high-polluting sectors.

In order to extend analysis to those questions that involve *inter*country-feedback effects, it is very appealing for the future to integrate the environmental module of the AET model into a multicountry framework. There is such a potential (in accordance with which choice of structure and software environment in GAMS was made) with respect to the one multicountry model currently available that has a distinct Austrian part, the Habsburg CGE model (focusing on Austria, Hungary, and the EC).[42]

[42] Hinojosa-Ojeda, Robinson and Tesche (1992).

VI

CONCLUSIONS

1. Categorizing the Issues

For environmental policy influencing trade flows three relevant modes of environmental regulation need to be distinguished: product regulation, production process regulation, and - particularly as a subcase of the latter - allocation of environmental control costs. Product regulation generally enhances the domestic market position of domestic production, while process regulation may reduce the domestic position in international markets. To mitigate the latter effects subsidies to cover environmental control costs are discussed.

For the impact trade liberalization exerts on the state of the environment, the crucial parameter is the level of environmental policy in effect in the respective countries. Therefore, the true question is whether for countries in a situation of further trade liberalization it is both legally allowed and politically feasible to implement environmental policy at a level considered otherwise necessary.

Further issues, for methodological reasons only cursorily covered in the present study, concern the appropriateness of trade bans to save endangered species, the successfullness of trade policy as an enforcement instrument for environmental agreements, and trade implications of international environmental initiatives.

2. Current International Regulation

The regulatory body which is far further developed is that of international trade. The main discussion therefore revolves around the GATT, but also the guidelines the OECD put forward in 1972 in its "Guiding Principles Concerning the International Economic Aspects of Environmental Policy" as well as new guidelines discussed to date. Serving as an international example, and of particular relevance for a European country is EU regulation.

The GATT and the OECD guidelines closely correspond in their spirit, though while the OECD mentioned environmental concerns explicitly already in 1972, the GATT will do so only whith the implementation of the Uruguay Round Final Act. For product regulation the body of actual legal relevance, GATT, currently grants countries wide latitude in independent regulation, the only requirements being equal treatment of domestic and imported products (non-discrimination) and equal treatment of all imported products irrespective of their origin (most-favored nation clause). A supplementary agreement to GATT of 38 signatories in 1993, the Agreement on Technical Barriers to Trade (Standards Code), while generally laying down harmonization of regulations for products explicitly allows product regulation for environmental ends to differ. It only requests information of the secretariat and also provides a procedure for the settlement of disputes. Within the Uruguay Round Final Act signed on April 15, 1994, the Standards Code is extended to all GATT contracting parties. In this regard also a clearer definition of the Code with respect to a proportionality requirement between the environmental objective and trade-restricting effects was discussed within the Uruguay Round negotiations, but has been slated to a future work program. It is to be expected that for product regulation the international regulatory development may move from currently wide latitude towards stronger restriction of country independence, but that quite a range of latitude will nonetheless remain.

Of generally higher interest and more controversial is the second area, that of production process regulation. The GATT obviously does allow for divergency in environmental process regulation across countries, but does not allow for any measures intended to counterbalance price differentials arising, be it import tariffs on foreign products produced under laxer standards or subsidies for domestic production to cover nationally higher environmental control costs. However, within the Uruguay Round Final Agreement there was a last minute change to respect subsidies up to a 20 percent fraction of investment costs due to new environmental regulation as non-countervailable. The exceptions to the general GATT principles contained in Article XX are being discussed as to whether they should be explicitly extended to measures taken for environmental ends. In environmental dispute panel cases up to date the exceptions have been interpreted narrowly, GATT panels not considering themselves the appropriate body to rule on the environmental merits of any measures such that they might weigh them against trade-impedement effects. The trade and environment issues are given emphasis in the work of the new institutional framewok of GATT, the World Trade Organization, with a Subcommitte of its´ Preparatory Committe already having gone to work in continuing the discussions of the former GATT working group on "Environmental Measures and International Trade".

In EU regulation no equivalent to the "national treatment clause" exists. Therefore any environmental product regulation can be considered to be in contradiction to Article 30 of the Treaty of Rome ensuring the free movement of goods among EU member countries. The European Court ruling in the Danish bottle case in 1988 for these cases, however, has introduced a proportionality consideration, in the particular Danish case granting the environmental measure of a reuse-requirement of soft drink and beer bottles to override any trade considerations.

The distinctive feature of the EU is its large body of common environmental regulation, currently almost 300 directives and regulations. Since the mid-eighties only a qualified majority is necessary for common product regulation, while for common production process regulation full consensus among its members is still required. The latter is intended to particularly protect the southern countries against regulation they consider too tough and has been used repeatedly by some of them to block tightening of common process regulation. Countries are allowed to implement individually more stringent levels than the Union harmonized level, lower ones only in temporary exceptions. Implementation of the directives, however, has been slow in some countries, such that effectively in many cases already the exactly complying countries observe stricter regulation than their within-EU trading partners.

3. Trade and Environment in the Theoretical Framework

In the standard analysis trade liberalization can only cause environmental damage connected to welfare losses if environmental policy in one or both of the trading partner countries is set insufficiently. For non-transboundary pollution arising out of production it will be the country exporting the environmentally relevant good that suffers the welfare loss, for pollution connected to consumption, the importing country. In both cases the loss can be below or beyond the "traditional" (i.e. not reflecting environmental changes) welfare gains due to trade, determining an overall net gain or loss for the respective country.

This standard model can be criticized (Tudini, 1993) on the basis of its assumption of full substitutability between environmental resources and other input factors as well as on the methodological valuation controversies and effective political undervaluation of environmental resources that cause "perverse implications of free trade"[1].

In consideration of these shortcomings it has on the other hand to be acknowledged that trade restrictions, for what purpose ever they are

[1] Tudini (1993), p. 18.

implemented, always also involve a decrease in welfare that could otherwise be accrued by international division of labor.

This dichotomy forms the basis of current discussion on the appropriateness of trade measures for environmental ends.

4. Trade Measures for Environmental Ends?

One evaluation criterion can be found in whether trade itself directly and strongly contributes to the environmental problem. One example where there is agreement on this being the case is hazardous waste disposal, the Basel Convention therefore seeking to ban exports where improper disposal is likely. More controversial is the case of tropical timber. On average, exports of tropical timber account for only 1 per cent of trees felled in developing countries, but in selected countries are of extraordinary significance, Malysia and Indonesia accounting for 75 per cent of world tropical timber exports. When trade is considered close to the root of the problem, proposals cover a range from the requirement of sustainable management certification up to trade bans.

A second criterion concerns the geographic scope of the environmental problem. While broader scope for trade measures is seen for global and transboundary problems, the case for national and local ones is highly controversial.

For global and transboundary problems the limitation of emissions by an individual country contains necessarily a public good element. Trade measures are sought as a means to (a) convince other countries to join an international environmental agreement, to (b) prevent other country´s actions from undermining one´s own environmental efforts and to (c) deny other countries economic gains from failing to follow such norms. Bans or border adjustment measures, however, cannot give rise to the optimal solution, as they affect only a (small) part of production of the low-regulating country and in their construction usually do not take into account externality effects accruing in third or fourth countries. For an optimal solution a multi-country (or respectively global) *environmental* agreement would be necessary. As the incentive structure to participate in such agreements is in most cases very weak, there is relatively broad consensus that trade measures are to be used to induce participation, with some authors pointing out that first other forms of inducements, such as technical and financial aid need to be similarly considered. There are also voices considering the speed of multilateral agreement on environmental action either too slow or at levels considered too low by some countries and who therefore consider it necessary that trade measures should also be able to be taken unilaterally. This would cause the trade off between environmental regulation and national share in world production to concern only export markets, but not domestic markets, thereby increasing the likelihood of environmental action.

For environmental problems in the national and local range the trade theory perspective is that of differences in environmental endowments and preferences being one of the very reasons for the benefits of international trade, therefore denying the need for any trade measures. There is a range of counterarguments against the implications of this view. Some economists argue against it out of political reasons fearing for a continuously smoothly functioning free trade system if such strongly voiced environmental concerns are not given weight (Uimonen and Whalley, 1994). Counterarguments from the environmental community concern (a) the avoidance of any further environmental damage (current economic cost-benefit-analysis is considered to undervalue environmental resources and such resulting in wrong overall societal benefit quantifications), (b) most problems being considered national at first glance, while truly having important international elements and (c) consumption structures which cause environmental effects in countries far away missing crucial observation feedback effects (related to the concept of the ecological footprint). Essentially the discussion is on politics either following the "fundamental" or the "urgent" (Sloterdijk, 1989), the first considering the national voicing of interests sufficient to install the right policy and therefore denying trade measures, while the "urgent" could turn out to also include trade interventions for this category of problems.

5. Paradigmatic Background

Ultimately, the explanation for the divergency and contrast among the various demands voiced that trade regulation should fulfill can best be found in the paradigmatic background on a more basic level, that of disagreement on the character of the relationship between economy and nature. Structuring the trade and environment interpretation according to the classification of Colby (1990), under the paradigm of frontier economics, the most important link between trade and environment is seen in trade fostering growth and generating the resources for environmental quality improvement. Under the paradigm of environmental protection, the emphasis also includes trade contributing to faster diffusion of environmentally preferable production technologies. Under the resource management paradigm, the emphasis shifts towards the necessity of some trade limitations, including contingency on domestic sustainable management practices, but also towards approving border adjustment measures to grant stronger incentives for national environmental action. Under the eco-development paradigm, based on the observation that ecological subsystems do run ecological deficits, but when they cause exceeding the aggregate sustainability levels they are no longer survivable, incentives towards stronger regional autonomy are emphasized. They include again sustainable-resource-management-certificate contingency in free trade, but proponents also put forward at present loose concepts of the trade system to be directly formalized in terms of carrying capacity.

With most views voiced in current political processes being already based on more than one paradigm, the full political spectrum covers all of them. The currently dominant ones in industrialized countries, however, unambigously are frontier economics and environmental protection (SUSTAIN, 1994, p. 106).

6. Further Regulatory Development

Differences in opinion on the appropriate regulatory trade framework being that broad, and especially since they are based rather on differences in the paradigmatic background, they will hardly be overcome by consensus following only one line of thought. While the international working groups have not yet reached final agreement, some conclusions can be drawn. For product regulations, as mentioned, country latitude will be narrowed, but will leave quite some scope for diverging standards. For process regulation it is foreseeable that in the future there will be more weight given to environmental concerns in trade regulation. While under current GATT regulation counterbalancing measures are effectively only allowed for one case, namely that of imposing equivalent charges on like products that carry a domestic tax (if levied directly on the product, and irrespective of its purpose being environmental or otherwise), in the future either countervailability might be explicitly introduced for more cases of environmental regulation or, most likely, allowance of subsidies for environmental ends will be extended beyond the 20% subsidies for investment due to new environmental regulation, which is first granted witihin the Uruguay Round Final Act. But it is more than unlikely that countervailability will be extended so far that it is permitted for all national environmental regulation.

Nations therefore also in the future will have the option of independently choosing stricter environmental process regulation in areas or to degrees that are not countervailable at the border. In the discussion of such policy then, the question of weighing potential (at least short term) competitive disadvantage effects of such policy, against potential long term effects and environmental effects will be crucial. As was put forward above, this question similarly is relevant for countries within the EU in spite of its broad harmonization in regulation.

7. Effects of Divergent Process Regulation

For trade in goods that are homogenous, the main causation actually runs along the line of comparative advantage within traditional trade theory, resulting in environmental policy reducing specialization in the emission-intensive goods by raising production costs for them. This link mainly is relevant between countries of stronger economic divergence, such as between Austria and Third World countries, but in many aspects also between Western and Central and Eastern Europe.

A much larger fraction of trade, though of - on an average unit basis - smaller environmental effects, takes place in the form of cross-hauling within the same sector among very similar countries. For these cases of product differentiation and non-unit returns to scale new trade theory reveals a multitude of effects unilateral environmental policy can trigger.

Models of economic geography point out that countries implementing stricter environmental policy earlier than others may gain first-mover benefits from the location decisions of new industries evolving internationally (clean industry sectors).

Markets of imperfect competition (resulting from product differentiation or increasing returns to scale) are characterized by rents, which can cause strategic behavior of agents to "grab" these rents. Strategic behavior on the side of producers results in socially inefficient overinvestement. Its size is influenced largely by environmental policy, in particular the instrument of environmental policy chosen. Initial partial analysis results for particular world markets point out that for the case of unilateral environmental action, the welfare benefits due to environmental policy can be roughly doubled when the tax instrument is chosen (versus standards), because this keeps overinvestment lower. For internationally coordinated environmental action the results are reversed, standards turning out to be superior to taxes. In imperfect competition settings, even the direction of price changes may be counterintuitive. For the country with stricter regulation, prices in the affected industries may fall when the location decision of firms is dominated by competitiveness considerations (Ulph A., 1992, 1993).

But governments also could act strategically. Being prohibited from many other forms of trade instruments, they may seek to use environmental policy to manipulate trade in imperfect competition settings. The direction and size of deviation from the otherwise optimal level of environmental policy depends on the instrument used and competition being in prices (Bertrand) or quantities (Cournot). For standards and quantity competition, they will be set weaker than otherwise (Ulph A., 1991).

Such theoretical and empirically calibrated (to particular world markets) models point out that imperfect competition does not mitigate the welfare effects of unilateral environmental action, but rather intensifies them (e.g. by additionally affecting strategic producer behavior), though now they can go both directions, dependent on the particular setting.

Empirical studies at the whole economy level have so far found the impacts of environmental regulation on both trade flows and firm location decisions to be very small, if present at all. For trade flows the main reason is the low share of environmental control costs in total costs and most countries having introduced environmental regulations at a similar speed. Major limitations of these studies concern the determination of environmental control costs (studies including indirect cost effects usually resulting in larger impacts), the time period (studies mainly focused on data from the 60´s and 70´s with relatively low regulation and lower economic openness), and the neglect of benefits arising (environmental, but also increases in innovation, health and productivity due to environmental policy). For the time ahead, substantial increases in environmental control costs are to be expected in selected sectors. At the specific industry level there are already currently studies and company surveys that point out environmental regulation levels to be non-negligible in the location decision.

8. The Case of Austria

Also for Austria, found by the German Institute of Economic Research to be the country with the highest share of environmental expenditures in GNP (UBA, 1993), environmental control costs (ECC) as a percentage of total costs rose slightly up to the early eighties, but still remain relatively low on an overall economy average (at 2.1 % in 1991). They vary strongly across sectors, but reach levels beyond 5% only in the petroleum industry, which is strongly protected. Four more strongly exposed sectors follow (chemicals, paper production, base metals and leather production), experiencing ECC in the range of 3.8 to 4.9 %, while the bulk of remaining sectors experiences them in the range of 0-2%. While these calculations are based on soft survey data (see section IV.3.1. also for its methodological limitation), it nevertheless gives some indication - comparing it with one other reference level among many - that for most goods categories import tariff protection is higher than potential competitive disadvantage by ECC. For some basic goods (characterized by low tariff rates) ECC exceed import tariffs.

Actual observation of trade flows avoids the statistical limitations in determing ECC and their divergencies across countries. Trade data analysis on the three digit SITC level for the period 1965-1988 (Low and Yeats, 1992) shows for the 40 product groups of highest ECC for Austria an index value of relative world market share of 1.57, indicating that Austria actually experiences - contrary to standard belief - an export specialization in environmentally heavily regulated industries, which also holds true when base metals trade flows, where subsidization might be considered to improve their export position, are not regarded.

The environmental goods and services sector merits seperate treatment. Trade performance within this sector is generally considered to be enhanced by early and strict national environmental regulation. For an actual evaluation of the trade performance, technologies have to be distinguished as to whether they are standardized, implying strong price competition (e.g. desulfurization equipment), or not. The latter category is of particular relevance in the environmental sector and its role is expected to further increase with the switch from end-of-pipe approaches to integrated solutions. Environmental goods and services markets are considered the growth markets of the 90s. To date, empirical analysis reveals Austria to experience both comparative advantage and export specialization in this sector, in particular in the segments of air pollution reduction and waste water treatment equipment.

9. Empirical Quantification of the Economic Effects of Unilateral Environmental Action

From the survey on the theoretical approaches it became evident that for sectors characterized by product differentiation various opposing effects of unilaterally more stringent environmental policy can be observed, while for those sectors of primarily homogenous goods characterization, environmental regulation causes almost unidirectional competitive disadvantage.

This effectively larger concern with strongly exposed basic industry sectors that follows from the theoretical discussion of unilateral environmental policy also carries over to the political discussion. This is especially so when substantial whole economy wide regulation is discussed, further enhanced for the case of Austria by its large share of basic industries.

In view of this focus, the model structure has been chosen, distinguishing between exposed (and usually simultanously of high pollution intensity) and sheltered and non-trading sectors. For the exposed sectors, additionally old production capital is distinguished from capital arising from new investment.

The methodology has been chosen based on conclusions about the limitations of earlier trade and environment studies. The focus on only historical data has been regarded as insufficient for adequate predictions on future development, inclusion of indirect costs has been identified as crucial, and benefits have been found to be hardly covered. Therefore (a) a simulation approach has been chosen that (b) fully covers indirect effects and, (c) while not focusing on benefits, allows their inclusion.

The Austrian Environment and Trade computable general equilibrium (CGE) model thereby can build on recent European modeling experience, particularly on a model of the Swedish economy (Bergman, 1991). A single-country model is constructed for comparative static analysis. The Austrian economy is aggregated into three exposed (base metals, chemicals, and paper and wood) and four sheltered and non-trading sectors (manufacturing, sheltered industries, services, public services) and the energy sector. Primary input factors cover labor, capital, fuels and electricity. A nested CES production structure allows for divergency in primary factor elasticities of substitution. Exposed sectors are modeled as world market price takers, while the remaining sectors experience some price-setting power (Armington-assumption). For environmental policy the example of CO_2 emission reduction policy has been chosen, implemented in the model in the form of a tradeable permits market and environmental taxes, each representative for any economically efficient policy instrument.

Based on a Social Accounting matrix for 1990, and the respective sectoral, household and total energy and emission data, as well as assumptions on time behavior data (productivity changes, factor growth, elasticities) based on the Austrian and international literature, a base case for the year 2005 has been calculated as the reference scenario.

In policy simulation the unilateral introduction of CO_2 policy to keep emissions constant at the 1990 level (a stringency level discussed within the EU, but apparently far from agreement) results in substantial output reduction in one of the exposed sectors (exceeding 50%). Relative factor prices shift towards an increase in the electricity price and a slight decrease in labor, with constant capital price (as there are larger substitution possibilities between labor and energy than capital and energy). Model results also supply the marginal cost of abatement for

CO_2 emission stabilization at 0,26 AS/kg CO_2. In combination with surveys on technology costs (Hofer, 1993) this allows determination of which of these technologies pay in such a scenario (e.g. district heating does, while obviously solar technology at current cost levels does not).

The question arising is whether the strong effects on the exposed sectors can be mitigated. A proposal discussed is exempting these sectors from environmental policy. The counterargument is, however, that because they are the most pollution intensive sectors, stringency levels in the other sectors would then need to be particularly severe to meet the environmental objective, thereby creating strong indirect effects on the exposed sectors that might largely offset initial exemption. The AET model for this analysis covers indirect effects via both intermediate inputs (input-output-table) and primary factor markets (price changes).

When environmental policy is sectorally differentiated in the AET model, exempting exposed sectors, and raising the emission tax level in the remaining sectors to reach CO_2 emission stabilization, the results indicate that this indeed can almost fully mitigate output reduction in exposed sectors that would arise in the case of unilateral, but sectorally uniform environmental policy. Thus indirect effects are quantified to only slightly impact the international competitive position in the exposed sectors (much less than direct emission taxes). Relative price changes are observed to be much stronger in this case, as is input factor substitution towards capital. Primary factor market shifts, while stronger than in the uniform policy case, however, are effectively mitigated in the one category where they could be regarded as problematic due to more difficult adjustment, which is the labor market.

This basic result indicates that Austria, even in a world where counterbalancing measures on an environmental basis are not allowed, if it is concerned about exposed sectors, still can introduce unilaterally stricter environmental policy at its preferred level and avoid the decline of exposed sectors´ output by an appropriate policy shaping.

For a proper answer to the remaining question of comparing the effects of unilateral versus internationally coordinated policy in an open economy a multi-country-model is required. A link of the environmental AET module to such an existing multi-country model containing Austria, together with dynamization of the AET model to endogenize optimization on the resource development over time, is among the outlooks for future research with the AET model.

APPENDIX 1

Uruguay Round Decision on Trade and Environment [1]

Ministers, meeting on the occasion of signing the Final Act embodying the results of the Uruguay Round of Multilateral Trade Negotiations at Marrakesh on April 15,

Recalling the preamble of the Agreement establishing the World Trade Organization (WTO), which states that members´ "relations in the field of trade and economic endeavour should be conducted with a view to raising standards of living, ensuring full employment and a large and steadily growing volume of real income and effective demand, and expanding the production of and trade in goods and services, while allowing for the optimal use of the world´s resources in accordance with the objectives of sustainable development, seeking both to protect and preserve the environment and to enhance the means for doing so in a manner consistent with their respective needs and concerns at different levels of economic development,"

Noting:

- the Rio Declaration on Environment and Development, Agenda 21, and its follow-up in GATT, as reflected in the statements of the Chairman of the Council of Representatives to the CONTRACTING PARTIES at their 48th Session in December 1992, as well as the work of the Group on Environmental Measures and International Trade, the Committee on Trade and Development, and the Council of Representatives;

- the work programme envisaged in the Decision on Trade in Services and the Environment; and

- the relevant provisions of the Agreement on Trade-Related Aspects of Intellectual Property Rights,

Considering that there should not be, nor need be, any policy contradiction between upholding and safeguarding an open, non-discriminatroy and equitable multilateral trading system on the one hand, and acting for the protection of the environment, and the promotion of sustainable development on the other,

---

[1] Trade and Environment Decision of 14 April 1994, MTN.TNC/MIN(94)/1/Rev. 1

Desiring to coordinate the policies in the field of trade and environment, and this without exceeding the competence of the multilateral trading system, which is limited to trade policies and those trade-related aspects of environmental policies which may result in significant trade effects for its members,

Decide:

- to direct the first meeting of the General Council of the WTO to establish a Committee on Trade and Environment open to all members of the WTO to report to the first biennial meeting of the Ministerial Conference after the entry into force of the WTO when the work program and terms of reference of the Committee wil be reviewed, in the light of recommendations of the Committee,

- that the TNC Decision of 15 December 1993 which reads, in part, as follows:

"(a) to identify the relationship between trade measures and environmental measures, in order to promote sustainable development;

(b) to make appropriate recommendations on whether any modifications of the provisions of the multilateral trading system are required, compatible with the open, equitable and non-discriminatory nature of the system, as regards, in particular:

- the need for rules to enhance positive interaction between trade and environmental measures, for the promotion of sustainable development, with special consideration to the needs of developing countries, in particular those of the least developed among them; and
- the avoidance of protectionist trade measures, and the adherence to effective multilateral disciplines to ensure responsiveness of the multilateral trading system to environmental objectives set forth in Agenda 21 and the Rio Declaration, in particular Principle 12; and
- surveillance of trade measures used for environmental purposes, of trade-related aspects of environmental measures which have significant trade effects, and of effective implementation of the multilateral disciplines governing those measures,"

constitutes, along with the preambular language above, the terms of reference of the Committee on Trade and Environment,

- that, within these terms of reference, and with the aim of making international trade and environmental policies mutually supportive, the Committee will initially address the following matters, in relation to which any relevant issue may be raised:

- the relationship between the provisions of the multilateral trading system and trade measures for environmental purposes, including those pursuant to multilateral environmental agreements;
- the relationship between environmental policies relevant to trade and environmental measures with significant trade effects and the provisions of the multilateral trading system;
- the relationship between the provisions of the multilateral trading system and:

(a) charges and taxes for environmental purposes

(b) requirements for environmental purposes relating to products, including standards and technical regulations, packaging, labelling and recycling;

- the provisions of the multilateral trading system with respect to the transparency of trade measures used for environmental purposes and environmental measures and requirements which have significant trade effects;
- the relationship between the dispute settlement mechanisms in the multilateral trading system and those found in multilateral environmental agreements;
- the effect of environmental measures on market access, especially in relation to developing countries, in particular to the least developed among them, and environmental benefits of removing trade restrictions and distortions;
- the issue of exports of domestically prohibited goods,

- that the Committee on Trade and Environment will consider the work programme envisaged in the Decision on Trade in Services and the Environment and the relevant provisions of the Agreement on Trade-Related Aspects of Intellectual Porperty Rights as an integral part of its work, within the above terms of reference,

- that, pending the first meeting of the General Council of the WTO, the work of the Committee on Trade and Environment should be carried out by a Sub-Committee of the Preparatory Committee of the World Trade Organization (PCWTO), open to all members of the PCWTO,

- to invite the Sub-Committee of the Preparatory Committee, and the Committee on Trade and Environment when it is established, to provide input to the relevant bodies in respect of appropriate arrangements for relations with inter-governmental and non-governmental organizations referred to in Article V of the WTO.

APPENDIX 2

Environmental Policy Shifting the General Equilibrium Supply Curves in a Trade Model

First the effect of environmental policy on the production possibility frontier has to be depicted. Following Wießner (1991), chapter 3, one way of modeling is to let (binding) environmental policy cause inward shifts in the production possiblity frontier. For the production of the externality creating commodity resources now have to be shifted away from direct production towards cleaning activities. Therefore, for everything else constant, relatively less of the polluting commodity can be produced, the production possiblity frontier is shifted inwards for the polluting commodity. Production possibility of the "clean" commodity is not affected. (Figure A.1)

In Figure A.2 the general equilibrium supply curves are derived from the production possibilty frontier by the construction of tangents representing a relative price ration p_2/p_1 (which equals the steepness, tan ß). For each price ratio then the according amounts of commodities 1 and 2 supplied can be depicted. The production choice at point E is triggered by a price ration p_E, at point H by p_H.

When the production possibilty frontier is shifted inwards due to environmental policy, the same steepness of the tangent (the same price ratio p_2/p_1) implies a lower amount of commodity 1 produced and a higher amount of commodity 2 respectively (point G). For the commodity whose production causes a negative externality the supply curve shifts inwards. A result which is used in section III.2.

Figure A.1: Production Possibility Frontier

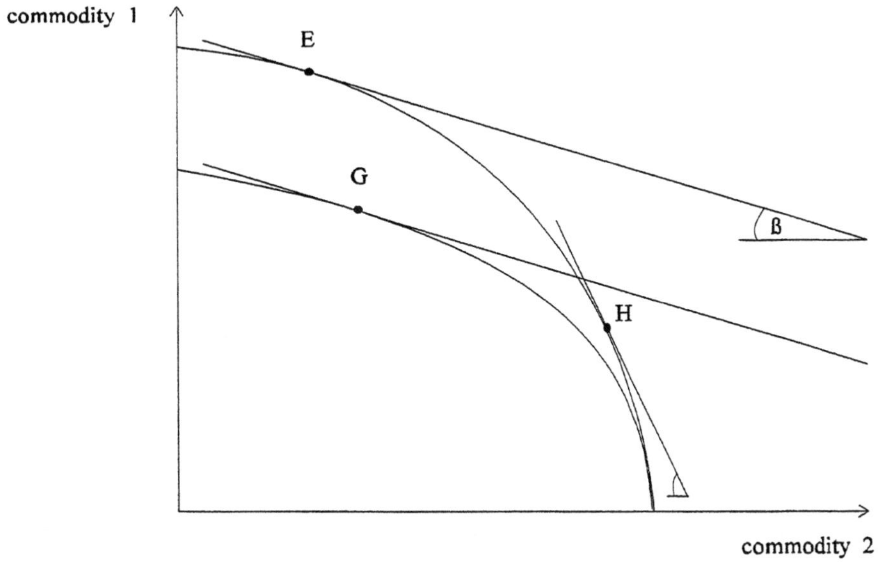

Figure A.2: Shifts in Suply Curves for Both Commodities for One Country following Environmental Policy

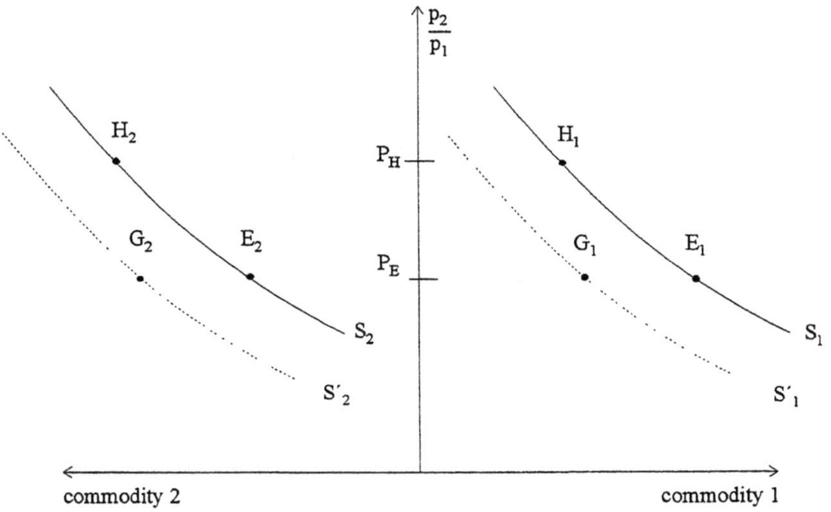

APPENDIX 3

A Schematic Social Accounting Matrix

This appendix is to give a brief introduction to the construction of a Social Accounting Matrix (SAM) and its use as a data basis for CGE modeling. It is based on lecture notes by Shanta Devarajan, John F. Kennedy School of Government, Harvard University.

The Social Accounting Matrix is the synthesis of two well-known ideas in economics. The first stems from the input-output-table: the purchase of an intermediate input by one sector is the sale of that same input by another sector. This transaction only enters in one cell in the input-ouptu-table, while it enters in the balance sheet of two different sectors in double-entry bookkeeping. In the SAM this idea is generalized to all transactions in the economy. Any flow of money, say, a household to a productive sector (a purchase of that sector's output by the household) is recorded in the cell whose row is that sector and column is the household.

The second idea derives from national income accounting, and is that income equals expenditure. While national income accountants make this claim for the economy as a whole, the same is true for each productive sector, worker, household and institution. That is, for the agricultural sector, its income from sales must equal its total expenditure on inputs, labor, imports etc. Traditionally, this is expressed as the equality between the two sides of the ledger in double-entry bookkeeping. Here, it is expressed as the requirement, that the row sum (income) equal the column sum (expenditure). The convention is adopted, that incomes are recorded along the rows and outlays along the columns. This equality between row and column sums will be used to represent the budget constraints for the CGE model.

One other issue needs to be resolved, before the schematic SAM can be read. There is a distinction between activities and commodities for two reasons. First, this allows for having more than one type of activity producing the same commodity. For example, small- and large-scale farmers may produce the same agricultural commodity (food). Yet, their technologies may be quite different. This framework allows to seperate their technologies in the activities column, yet combine their output in the commodities account. Second, the treatment of imports is always a problem in these types of schemata. If imports are in any way competitive with domestically produced goods, then domestic demand will consist of both types of goods. However, exports will continue to be only of the domestically produced variety. Separating activity accounts from commodities enables to depicture this circumstance.

Figure A.3: A Schematic Social Accounting Matrix

	Activi-ties	Com-modities	Factors	House-hold	Gov´t	Capital	Rest of World
Activities		Domestic Sales					Exports
Com-modities	Inter-mediate Inputs			Private Con-sumption	Gov´t Con-sumption	Invest-ment	
Factors	Value added						
House-hold			Allocat-ion Matrix		Gov´t Transfers		
Gov´t	Indirect Taxes	Import Tariffs		Income Taxes			
Capital				Private Savings	Gov´t Savings		Foreign Savings
Rest of World	Imports						

Reading across the activity row, then, it is observed that its total income comes from exports and sales to the commodity account. The commodity account can be thought of as a "supermarket" that carries both foreign and domestic goods. The column of the activity row contains its expenditures: on intermediate inputs, value added and indirect taxes. Note, that the sum of these should equal gross output. The commodity account buys domestic products from the activity account and imports from the rest of the world. In turn, it pays the import tariffs to the government (although, in effect, the consumer is paying it becasue the market price is correspondingly higher). The total supplies of the commodity account are then demanded by all domestic purchasers: intermediate, household, government and investment. The value added that accrues to factors in the activity account is allocated to households according to their endowment shares. Households, in turn, spend this income (as well as transfers from the government) on consumption and taxes; the residual is saved. The government, similarly, receives income from taxes - indirect taxes, tariffs and income taxes - and spends it on consumption, transfers and savings. The last two rows and columns reflect the familiar national accounts identities. The capital account row and column capture the equality between savings - private, government and foreign - with investment. The rest of the world account reflects the identity between the trade deficit (imports minus exports) and foreign savings.

The last three rows and columns are often labeled as reflecting the three "macro-balances". In the specification of a Computable General Equilibrium Model one of their equation sides has to be left endogenous, such that it can adjust to ensure equilibrium. Which one is chosen, then defines the so called closure of the model. For example, for the capital account a "classical" closure would mean that investment is inherently model determined (e.g. dependent on current period output growth) and then savings is set equal to that amount of investment, whereas a Keynesian closure would work the other way round, savings representing a residual of income and then driving investment.

APPENDIX 4

Tables

Table A.1. Austrian Environmental Expenditures by Industry Sector

	Env. Exp. as % of production value [%]			Env. Exp. as % of value added [%]		Environmental Expenditures [mio. AS]		
	1985	1988	1991	1985	1988	1985	1988	1991
Mining	2,79	2,36	1,87	4,40	4,32	252,3	207,0	154,1
Ferrous metals production	4,01	4,45	3,79	7,52	8,33	1.188,5	1.319,3	945,8
Mining and ferrous metals	3,73	3,97	3,32	6,69	7,40	1.440,7	1.526,3	1.099,9
Petro	4,03	8,63	7,44	18,30	17,04	1.884,2	1.681,4	1.601,5
Stone and Ceramics	2,31	2,02	2,66	4,82	4,11	532,4	531,4	779,7
Glass	0,72	1,96	1,83	1,15	3,15	51,4	141,1	160,6
Chemicals	2,92	2,96	4,89	8,86	7,62	2.374,8	2.570,5	4.410,6
Paper production	2,47	3,83	4,39	10,24	14,36	776,6	1.397,2	1.703,3
Paper processing	0,77	1,20	0,80	2,38	3,47	78,2	134,5	113,9
Audiovision	0,06	0,28	0,32	0,11	0,51	1,1	8,6	13,3
Wood processing	1,00	0,81	3,18	2,34	1,93	192,5	190,0	972,1
Food	0,46	0,62	0,93	1,09	1,39	398,4	542,3	967,9
Leather production	2,45	1,49	4,39	16,87	6,33	46,9	23,5	84,9
Leather processing	0,37	0,17	0,24	0,94	0,43	29,9	10,9	14,9
Foundries	0,94	1,68	3,23	1,86	3,22	60,2	119,7	263,7
Nonferrous metals	0,55	0,58	1,54	2,45	2,53	99,9	111,9	254,8
Machinery and steel construction	0,51	0,60	0,70	1,02	1,21	334,6	424,8	684,2
Vehicles	0,72	0,77	1,36	1,69	1,92	237,5	280,5	703,0
Metal manufacturing	0,58	0,77	1,10	1,28	1,63	247,6	355,0	587,4
Electro and Electronics	0,54	0,38	0,50	0,94	0,73	263,4	231,8	418,4
Textiles	0,94	0,57	0,83	2,21	1,32	260,3	162,6	272,9
Clothing	0,45	0,45	0,48	1,10	1,07	65,7	65,6	72,0
Gas and heating	1,55	15,78	3,55	9,57	68,88	428,9	3.023,7	981,0
Total	1,53	2,08	2,10	3,80	4,78	9.805,2	13.533,3	16.160,0

Sources: Environmental Expenditures: Bundeskammer der Gewerblichen Wirtschaft (1992), Aufwendungen der Industrie für den Umweltschutz,p. 38 and Table 46BH in Bundeskammer der Gewerblichen Wirtschaft (1986, 1989, 1992).
Production Values: Österreichisches Statistisches Zentralamt (1986, 1989, 1992), Industrie- und Gewerbestatistik,, 1. Teil, Tables 4(later 5).1.12.
Value added: Österreichisches Statistisches Zentralamt (1987, 1991), Industriestatistik 1985, 1988, 2. Teil, Tab. 5, p. 12.

For interpretation see section IV.3.1.

Tab. A.2. Sectoral Decomposition AET Model

AET-model		standard 19-sector specification (WIFO)
[1]	Basemet	10
[2]	Chemic	7
[3]	Papwood	5+6
[4]	Manuf	4+9+11
[5]	Shelt	1+3+13
[6]	Serv	2+8+12+14+15+16+17+18
[7]	Publ	19

with

1	Agriculture and forestry
2	Mining
3	Food
4	Textil
5	Wood
6	Paper
7	Chemicals
8	Petro
9	Stone and Ceramics
10	Base metals
11	Metal manufacturing
12	Energy and water supply
13	Building and construction
14	Commerce
15	Lodging
16	Transport
17	Banking
18	Other services
19	Public services

Tab. A.3. Foreign Trade

	Exports	Imports	Net-Exports
Agriculture and Forestry	10,165	31,399	-21,234
Mining	1,004	14,272	-13,268
Food	22,160	35,237	-13,077
Textil	45,656	47,737	-2,081
Wood	51,533	24,744	26,789
Paper	53,537	32,597	20,940
Chemicals	62,500	69,023	-6,523
Petro	20,389	45,016	-24,627
Stone	27,563	19,956	7,607
Base Metals	51,693	45,124	6,569
Metals	212,726	292,224	-79,498
Energy	13,824	3,491	10,333
Building and Construction	6,583	1,75	4,833
Commerce	56,938	19,886	37,052
Lodging	0,127	3,216	-3,089
Transport	77,769	20,197	57,572
Banking	6,220	5,784	0,436
Other Services	0,788	0,457	0,331
Public Sector	3,136	1,878	1,258
Sum	724,311	713,988	

Tab. A.4. Sectoral Energy Expenses

	energy consumption 1988 [TJ]	energy expenditures 1988 [mio AS], excl VAT hard coal	coke	soft coal	biketts	liquid gas	gasoline	petroleum	diesel oil	gasoil
Agriculture and Forestry	73245	206,50	244,53	101,20	75,57	17,98	317,63	0,00	1.619,21	111,83
Mining	6531	0,00	2,95	0,35	2,16	0,66	2,54	0,00	50,62	1,30
Food	20939	3,07	7,85	4,18	0,39	15,53	158,29	0,00	252,37	31,45
Textil	8011	0,86	1,43	0,27	0,33	2,44	52,79	0,00	16,61	6,39
Wood	12694	0,00	2,66	3,15	0,79	0,00	180,47	0,00	240,97	5,95
Paper	43021	3,16	0,34	41,23	26,57	7,23	53,38	0,00	26,75	1,75
Chemicals	27789	12,75	17,38	7,01	0,00	5,39	62,09	0,00	68,34	8,23
Petro	350	0,00	0,00	0,00	0,00	0,00	3,85	0,00	36,84	0,00
Stone	36223	198,76	34,45	24,31	0,61	34,24	120,31	0,00	539,81	13,33
Base Metals	86374	5,71	1.333,98	0,00	0,00	32,93	7,38	0,00	50,78	0,40
Metals	25748	2,27	4,51	0,82	0,71	48,75	531,06	0,00	243,69	33,42
Energy	1860	0,00	0,00	0,00	0,00	0,00	42,71	0,00	40,77	0,40
Building and Construction	12507	1,20	2,10	0,45	0,64	45,26	327,61	2,40	842,20	56,99
Commerce (and stock keeping)	22250	9,39	18,70	3,84	15,08	18,33	726,68	0,00	833,15	99,92
Lodging	17758	10,15	16,54	6,47	4,22	60,25	102,18	0,00	21,63	95,55
Transport (not incl. stock keeping)	56403	9,74	13,70	2,45	1,73	84,63	300,73	1.115,20	5.067,67	63,56
Banking	4808	0,59	1,81	0,17	0,26	1,30	180,91	0,00	24,99	22,47
Other Services	26029	1,08	32,09	17,49	1,02	11,30	87,72	0,00	145,66	56,51
Public Sector	11689	2,47	23,75	24,74	2,54	1,75	155,37	91,71	220,62	42,50
Private Consumption	309867	248,18	1 895,02	234,78	780,78	142,60	22.969,90	196,35	1 749,64	4.157,89
SUM	803894,000	715,88	3.653,79	472,91	913,40	530,57	26 383,80	1.405,86	12.092,32	4.809,84

	fuel oil a o oil	city gas	gas	refinery gas	district heatin	electricity	SUM
Agriculture and Forestry	388,63	0,00	71,40	0,00	0,59	1 828,74	2.694,45
Mining	72,53	0,00	151,56	0,00	2,10	311,38	60,58
Food	409,72	1,03	288,03	0,00	45,70	1 471,97	473,13
Textil	139,42	0,00	114,62	0,00	7,15	762,86	81,12
Wood	83,49	0,00	58,25	0,00	10,27	1 021,62	433,99
Paper	233,05	0,00	439,27	0,00	20,85	2.152,05	160,41
Chemicals	208,12	0,00	344,92	11,50	25,64	2.391,89	181,19
Petro	0,00	0,00	0,00	0,00	0,00	9,26	40,69
Stone	317,96	2,17	415,52	0,67	4,90	1.596,26	965,82
Base Metals	278,40	0,00	552,75	813,99	2,44	2.706,37	1.431,18
Metals	312,91	0,00	416,97	0,00	135,61	2.599,50	865,23
Energy	1,90	0,31	0,69	0,00	8,41	354,90	83,88
Building and Construction	151,36	0,00	37,96	0,00	4,85	447,50	1 278,85
Commerce (and stock keeping)	361,22	1,41	199,86	0,00	87,34	2.395,47	1.725,09
Lodging	703,15	2,95	110,92	0,00	84,17	2.115,18	316,99
Transport (not incl stock keeping)	114,21	0,00	102,23	0,00	268,54	3 065,78	6.659,41
Banking	75,04	1,19	74,32	0,00	98,37	698,72	232,50
Other Services	441,01	14,78	477,10	0,00	824,13	2.193,68	352,87
Public Sector	151,09	3,32	119,85	0,00	272,59	1.012,39	565,45
Private Consumption	163,13	80,60	4.434,84	0,00	1 626,34	14.020,76	32 375,14
SUM	4 604,34	107,76	8 411,06	826,16	3 529,99	43.156,26	50 977,97

Source: transformed to 19-sector specification from ÖSTAT (1992b), Monetäre Aufwendungen für den energetischen Endverbrauch im Jahr 1988

Total energy use also includes firewood, combustible wastes and direct water power use (comprising a share of 4,28% of Austrian energy expenditure).

Tab. A.5. Sectoral Energy Expenses 1990 Estimates

	energy expenses 1990 estimated*) [mio. AS], excl. VAT				
	coal	gas	oil, gasoline	district	electricity
Agriculture and Forestry	674,58	69,76	2.533,98	0,56	1.961,65
Mining	6,48	148,07	128,35	2,00	333,99
Food	16,25	282,22	879,41	43,42	1.578,95
Textil	3,16	111,98	217,71	6,79	818,30
Wood	6,88	56,91	525,69	9,76	1.095,87
Paper	75,39	429,17	321,62	19,81	2.308,46
Chemicals	38,82	348,49	354,03	24,36	2.565,73
Petro	0,00	0,00	42,41	0,00	9,93
Stone	261,80	408,35	1.056,06	4,66	1.712,27
Base Metals	1.515,82	1.354,03	375,43	2,32	2.903,06
Metals	9,06	407,38	1.207,18	128,83	2.788,42
Energy	0,00	0,92	89,00	7,99	380,69
Building and Construction	4,83	37,09	1.484,88	4,61	480,02
Commerce (and stock keeping)	53,80	196,38	2.100,82	82,97	2.569,57
Lodging	40,28	110,71	991,60	79,96	2.268,91
Transport (not incl. stock keeping)	31,93	107,07	7.128,34	273,48	3.288,59
Banking	3,14	73,55	311,47	93,45	749,50
Other Services	54,47	477,85	746,05	782,92	2.353,11
Public Sector	54,94	119,73	647,50	258,96	1.085,97
Private Consumption	3.627,41	4.396,75	30.390,29	1.545,02	15.039,75
Private Consumption incl. VAT	4.352,89	5.276,11	36.468,35	1.854,03	18.047,70
SUM (excl. Priv Cons)	2.851,59	4.739,66	21.141,50	1.826,84	31.252,99
SUM (excl. VAT)	6.479,00	9.136,41	51.531,80	3.371,86	46.292,74

*) increase in quantity of total fossil energy per sector (assuming constant mix between coal, gas and oil) according to UBA (1992),CO2-Emissionsentwicklung, p. 6; increases 1988-1990: transport + 7,24%, other industry sectors and private consumption net increase balanced

increase in quantity of electricty according to total demand increase by 7,27%, assumed equal over all sectors and private consumption

total demand increase: source ÖSTAT (1990,1992a), Energieversorgung Österreichs,
increase in prices per kind of energy calculated from ÖSTAT (1990,91), op. cit., Tab. 7.3.

Tab. A.6. Energy Expenses AET-Model Structure

		coal	gas	oil	district heat	electricity
[1]	Basemet	1.515,82	1.354,03	375,43	2,32	2.903,06
[2]	Chemic	38,82	348,49	354,03	24,36	2.565,73
[3]	Papwood	82,26	486,08	847,31	29,56	3.404,32
[4]	Manuf	274,02	927,72	2.480,95	140,28	5.319,00
[5]	Shelt	695,65	389,07	4.898,26	48,58	4.020,62
[6]	Serv	190,09	1.114,56	11.538,03	1.322,78	11.954,29
[7]	Publ	54,94	119,73	647,50	258,96	1.085,97
	[Sum]	2.851,59	4.739,66	21.141,50	1.826,84	31.252,99
	Private Cons. (excl. VAT)					15.039,75
	Private Cons. VAT					3.007,95
	Private Cons.					18.047,70
	Sum					49.300,70

Tab. A.7. Electricity Supply and Demand

[GWh]	1988	1989	1990	1991
generation	49.024	50.174	50.413	51.476
hydroelectric	36.540	36.146	32.492	32.725
caloric	12.484	14.028	17.921	18.751
imports	5.572	5.913	6.839	8.503
total supply	54.597	56.086	57.252	59.980
exports	8.283	8.245	7.298	7.738
pump storage	1.072	1.249	1.425	1.570
domestic demand	45.241	46.593	48.529	50.672
CO2-emissions from electricity production [mio. t]	8,004	9,017	11,519	

Sources: ÖSTAT (1990, 1991, 1992a), Energieversorgung Österreichs, Jahreshefte 1989-1991

UBA (1992), CO2-Emissionsentwicklung und Prognose für Österreich, p. 6.

Tab. A.8. National Fossil Fuel Energy Supply - Domestic and Imported

[GJ]

domestic fuels	121.870.877	valuation in AET:	total fuel use	67.147
imported fuels	748.011.276			
exported fuels	16.493.824		domestic supply	9.589
share domestic/use	0,14280823			

source: ÖSTAT (1991), Energieversorgung Österreichs, Jahresheft 1990, p. 19, Tab. 1.2.

Tab. A.9. Labor Productivity

average yearly changes

sector	period	%change	most recent %change
Agriculture and forestry	68-87	4,93	2,16 (83-87)
Mining	75-87	4,02	
Food	74-87	2,89	2,05 (81-87)
Textil	73-87	2,96	
Wood	74-87	3,20	2,96 (81-87)
Paper	75-87	3,47	
Chemicals	73-87	4,90	
Petro	74-87	0,00	
Stone and ceramics	73-87	3,39	
Base metals	75-87	4,62	
Metal manufacturing	71-87	3,07	1,64 (84-87)
Energy and water supply	74-87	3,23	2,99 (81-87)
Building and construction	72-87	1,78	
Commerce	73-87	1,73	
Lodging	73-87	0,06	
Transport	74-87	3,20	2,36 (81-87)
Banking	71-87	2,06	
Other Services	75-87	0,31	
Public Services	73-87	0,00	

Source: own calculations, based on Lager (1993), p. 91.

average yearly labor productivity change
AET-disaggregation

[1]	Basemet	4,62
[2]	Chemic	4,90
[3]	Papwoo	3,20
[4]	Manuf	2,12
[5]	Shelt	1,86
[6]	Serv	1,68
[7]	Publ	0,00

aggregated from above table weighted by 1990 sectoral labor

Tab. A.10. Energy Productivity

	energy intensity		%change	% change
	1988	1974	1974-1988	productivity
	[kJ/S-BIP]	[kcal/S-BIP]	deflated	1974-1988
Agriculture and forestry	1493,0	311,0	58,01	-36,71
Mining	2260,0	494,7	50,37	-33,50
Food	369,0	173,0	-29,79	42,44
Textil	305,2	157,1	-36,06	56,39
Wood	436,0	180,0	-20,27	25,43
Paper	1477,9	330,1	47,36	-32,14
Chemicals	711,0	334,0	-29,93	42,72
Petro	12,7	n.a.	n.a.	n.a.
Stone and ceramics	1346,6	720,0	-38,44	62,44
Base metals	3212,0	1144,0	-7,59	8,21
Metal manufacturing	172,7	85,2	-33,28	49,88
Energy and water supply	41,0	18,0	-25,03	33,38
Building and construction	119,0	73,0	-46,34	86,37
Commerce	112,0	85,0	-56,63	130,57
Lodging	320,0	334,0	-68,46	217,11
Transport	580,0	716,0	-73,34	275,05
Banking	31,0	18,0	-43,31	76,41
Other Services	93,0	102,0	-69,99	233,22
Public Services	n.a.	43,0	n.a.	n.a.

average yearly energy productivity change
AET-disaggregation

[1]	Basemet	0,565
[2]	Chemic	2,573
[3]	Papwood	-1,210
[4]	Manuf	3,197
[5]	Shelt	-0,044
[6]	Serv	8,106
[7]	Publ	8,980

aggregated from above, weighted by 1988 energy input per

REFERENCES - GENERAL :[1]

The epigraph is taken from John Stuart Mill, *On Liberty* (originally published in 1859), as quoted from J. S. Mill, *On Liberty and other writings*, ed. S. Collini (Cambridge texts in the history of economic thought), Cambridge: Cambridge University Press, 1989: p. 23.

Anderson, Kym, 1992, The standard welfare economics of policies affecting trade and the environment, in: Anderson and Blackhurst (1992): 25-48.

Anderson, Kym and Richard Blackhurst (eds.), 1992, *The Greening of World Trade Issues*, London: Harvester Wheatsheaf.

Arden-Clarke, Charles, 1991, The General Agreement on Tariffs and Trade, Environmental Protection and Sustainable Development, WWF-World Wide Fund for Nature-Discussion Paper, revised November.

Barbier, Edward B., 1989, *Economics, Natural-Resource Scarcity and Development: Conventional and Alternative Views*, London: Earthscan.

Barbier, Edward B., Joanne C. Burgess, T.M. Swanson and David W. Pearce, 1990, *Elephants, Economics and Ivory*, London: Earthscan.

Barbier, Edward B., Bruce A. Aylward, Joanne C. Burgess and Joshua T. Bishop, 1991, Environmental Effects of Trade in the Forestry Sector, paper prepared for the Joint Session of Trade and Environmental Experts, OECD Paris, draft, October.

---

[1] Exempts Chapter V (CGE) references, which have seperate reference section.

Barrett, Scott, 1992, Strategic Environmental Policy and International Trade, London Business School, mimeo, revised September.

Baumol, William and Wallace Oates, 1988, *The Theory of Environmental Policy*, Second Edition, Cambridge University Press.

Bendl, Erwin, 1993, *Motive der Standortwahl und Attraktivität des Industriestandortes Österreich*, Wien: Industriellenvereinigung, Dezember.

Bhagwati, Jagdish, 1991, *The World Trading System at Risk*, Princeton University Press.

Bohm, Peter and Bjorn Larsen, 1992, Fairness in a Tradeable-Permit Treaty for Carbon Emissions reductions in Europe and the former Soviet Union, paper prepared for the Environment Division of the EMENA Region, The World Bank, draft, October.

Bown, William, 1990, Trade Deals a Blow to the Environment, *New Scientist*, 10 November.

Breuss, Fritz (Koord.), 1993, *Die ökologischen Auswirkungen des Binnenmarktes auf Österreich*, Wien: Österreichisches Institut für Wirtschaftsforschung, Mai.

Breuss, Fritz and Jan Stankovsky, 1988, *Österreich und der EG-Binnenmarkt*, Institut für Angewandte Sozial- und Wirtschaftsforschung, Wien: Signum.

Bundeskammer der gewerblichen Wirtschaft, 1990, *Aufwendungen der Industrie für den Umweltschutz 1986-1995*, Abteilung für Statistik und Dokumentation, Wien.

_____, 1993, *Aufwendungen der Industrie für den Umweltschutz 1989-1995*, Abteilung für Statistik, Wien.

Burgess, Joanne C., 1991, Environmental Effects of Wildlife Trade on Endangered Species, paper prepared for the Joint Session of Trade and Environmental Experts, OECD Paris, draft, December 10.

Carraro, Carlo and Domenico Siniscalco, 1992, Environmental Innovation Policy and International Competition, *Environmental and Resource Economics*, Vol. 2: 183-200.

Carraro, Siniscalco and Giorgio Topa, 1992, Should Environmental Innovation Policy be Internationally Coordinated?, in: *Proceedings of the International Conference on "The International Dimension of Environmental Policy"*, Milano: Fondazione Enrico Mattei, October.

Chapman, Duane, 1991, Environmental Standards and International Trade in Automobiles and Copper: The Case for a Social Tariff, *Natural Resources Journal*, Vol. 31, winter: 449-461.

Charnovitz, Steve, 1993, Environmentalism Confronts GATT Rules. Recent Developments and New Opportunities, *Journal of World Trade*, Vol. 27, No. 2 (April): 37-54.

Cleveland, Cutler J., 1987, Biophysical Economics: Historical Perspectives and Current Research Trends, *Ecological Modelling*, 38: 47-73.

Colby, Michael E., 1990, *Environmental Management in Development: The Evolution of Paradigms*, World Bank Discussion Papers 80, Washington, D.C.: World Bank; republished 1991 in *Ecological Economics*, 3: 193-213.

Dean, Judith, 1992, Trade and The Environment: A Survey of the Literature, prepared for the World Bank, World Development Report 1992, April 1991; published in Low (1992): 15-28.

Faeth, Paul, Robert Repetto, Kim Kroll, Qi Dai, and Glenn Helmers (1991), *Paying the Farm Bill: U.S. Agricultural Policy and the Transition to Sustainable Agriculture*, Washington D.C.: World Resources Institute.

Farmer, Karl, Karl Steininger and Ronald Wendner, 1993, Nachhaltige Wirtschaftliche Entwicklung: Konzeptionen, Modellanalyse, Paradigmen von Wirtschaft-Natur-Beziehungen und umweltpolitische Anmerkungen, University of Graz, Department of Economics, research memorandum 9303.

Folke, Carl and Tomas Kaberger, 1991, Recent Trends in Linking the Natural Environment and the Economy, in: Folke and Kaberger (eds.), *Linking the Natural Environment and the Economy: Essay from the Eco-Eco Group*, Dordrecht: Kluwer: 273-300.

French, Hillary F., 1991, The EC: Environmental Proving Ground, *World Watch*, November-December: 26-33.

Gabel, H. Landis, 1992, Trade Liberalization, Transportation and the Environment, presented to the 3rd Annual Meeting of the European Association of Environmental and Resource Economists, Kraków, June.

Gandolfo, Giancarlo, 1987, *International Economics I: The Pure Theory of International Trade*, Berlin: Springer.

GATT Newsletter, 1991, GATT, the Uruguay Round and the Environment, FOCUS: GATT Newsletter 85, October.

GATT Secretariat, 1992, Trade and the Environment, in: *International Trade 90-91*, Geneva: GATT: 19-47.

GATT Trade Negotiations Committee, 1991, *Draft Final Act Embodying the Results of the Uruguay Round of Multilateral Trade Negotiations*, GATT Document MTN.TNC/W/FA, Dec. 20.

GATT Trade Negotiations Committee, 1994a, *Uruguay Round Final Act*, Marrakech, 15 April.

_____, 1994b, Trade and Environment, Decision of 14 April 1994, GATT Document MTN.TNC/MIN(94)/1/Rev. 1: 4-6.

Gavin, Joseph G. III, 1992, Environmental Protection and the GATT - A Business View, *The Columbia Journal of World Business*, Fall & Winter: 74-83.

Gronych, R., 1980, *Allokationseffekte und Außenhandelswirkungen der Umweltpolitik. Eine komparativ-statische Zwei-Sektor-Analyse*, Tübingen.

Grossman, Gene and Alan Krueger, 1991, Environmental Impacts of a North American Free Trade Agreement, Princeton University Working Paper, Princeton, NJ, October.

Hillard, Tom, 1991, Trade Advisory Committees: Privileged Access for Polluter, *Public Citizen's Congress Watch*, December.

Hoel, Michael, 1992a, How Should International Greenhouse Gas Agreements be Designed?, in: Dasgupta, Partha, Karl-Goran Mäler and Vercelli (eds.), *The Economics of Transnational Commons*, Oxford University Press.

_____, 1992b, International Environment Conventions: The Case of Uniform Reductions of Emissions, *Environmental and Resource Economics*, Vol. 2, No. 2, pp. 141-159.

Hofer, Markus, 1993, *Instrumente zur Reduktion der Kohlendioxid-Emissionen*, Grazer Schriftenreihe Verfahrenstechnik 5. Graz: dbv-Verlag für die Technische Universität Graz.

Hveem, Helge, 1992, Trade and the Environment: The International Political Economy, European University Institute, Working Group on Environmental Studies Seminar Paper, Florence: EUI, March.

Kalt, John, 1988, The Impact of Domestic Environmental Regulatory Policies on U.S. International Competitiveness, in: Spence, A. Michael and Heather A. Hazard (eds.), *International Competitiveness*, Cambridge, MA: Ballinger Publishing Co.

Keyes, Cameron, 1991, *The European Community and Environmental Policy: An Introduction for Americans*, Baltimore, MD: World Wildlife Publications.

Krutilla, Kerry, 1991, Environmental Regulation in an Open Economy, *Journal of Environmental Economics and Management*, Vol. 20: 127-142.

Krugman, Paul R., 1991, *Geography and Trade*, Cambridge, MA: MIT Press.

Layard, Richard and Alan Walters, 1978, *Microeconomic Theory*, New York: McGraw-Hill.

Legler, Harald, Hariolf Grupp, Birgit Gehrke and Ulrich Schasse, 1992, *Innovationspotential und Hochtechnologie*, Technologische Position Deutschalnds im Internationalen Wettbewerb, Heidelberg: Physica-Verlag.

Leonard, John, 1988, *Pollution and the Struggle for World Product: Multinational Corporations, Environment and International Comparative Advantage*, Cambridge, MA: Cambridge University Press.

Lesperance, Ann M., 1991, Air Quality Regulations and Their Impacts on Industrial Growth in California, Based on Census Data: A Case Study of the South Coast Air Quality Management District Rule 1136 and the Wood Products Coatings-Industry, master's degree thesis, University of California, Los Angeles.

Low, Patrick (ed.), 1992, *International Trade and the Environment*, World Bank Discussion Paper 159, Washington, D.C: The World Bank.

Low, Patrick and Alexander Yeats, 1992, Do "Dirty" Industries Migrate?, in: Low (1992): 89-104.

Markusen, J., E. Morey and N. Olewiler, 1991, Environmental Policy When Market Structure and Plant Location are Endogenous, *NBER Working Paper* 3671.

Martinez-Allier, Juan, 1987, *Ecological Economics: Economics, Environment, Society*, Oxford: Basil Blackwell.

Mirowski, Philip, 1989, *More Heat than Light: Economics as Social Physics, Physics as Nature's Economics*, Cambridge, MA: Cambridge University Press.

National Research Council, 1989, *Alternative Agriculture*, Washington, D.C.: National Academy Press.

Norgaard, Richard B., 1988, Sustainable Development: A Co-Evolutionary View, *Futures*, Vol. 20, No. 6: 606-620.

Oates, Wallace, Paul Portney and Arthur McGartland, 1989, The Benefits of Incentive-Based Regulations: A Case Study of Environmental Standard Setting, *American Economic Review*, Vol. 79: 1233-1242.

OECD, 1991, *The State of the Environment*, Paris: OECD, January.

OECD, 1993, *Environmental Policies and Industrial Competitiveness*, Paris: OECD.

Pearce, David W., and R. Kerry Turner, 1990, *Economics of Natural Resources and the Environment*, Baltimore: The Johns Hopkins University Press.

Pearce, David W., 1992, Should the GATT be Reformed for Environmental Reasons?, Centre for Social and Economic Research on the Global Environment, Working Paper GEC 92-06, London: University College.

Pearson, Charles and Robert Repetto, 1991, Reconciling Trade and Environment: The Next Steps, Johns Hopkins University/ World Resources Institute, prepared for The Trade and Environment Committee of the EPA, Washington, D.C., December.

Pearson, Charles, 1982, *Environmental Policies and Their Trade Implications for Developing Countries, with Special Reference to Fish and Shellfish, Fruit and Vegetables*, UNCTAD.

Petersmann, von Ernst Ulrich, 1992, Umweltschutz und Welthandelsordnung im GATT-, OECD- und EWG-Rahmen, *Europa-Archiv*, vol. 47, no. 9: 257-266.

Phipps, Thomas T., and K. Reichelderfer, 1988, *Agricultural Policy and Environmental Quality*, Washington, D.C: Resources for the Future.

Portney, Paul R. (ed.), 1990, Public Policies for Environmental Protection, Resources for the Future, Washington, D.C.

Rees, William R., 1992, Ecological Footprints and Appropriated Carrying Capacity: What Urban Econmics Leaves Out, *Environment and Urbanization* 4:2:121-130.

Reiterer, Michael, 1993, Das multilaterale Handelsystem und Internationaler Umweltschutz, *Wirtschaftspolitische Blätter* 3/4: 297.

_____, 1994, GATT/WTO: Internationaler Handel und Umwelt: Bilanz der GATT-Arbeitsgruppe über "Environmental Measures aand International Trade" (EMIT) sowie der Uruguay-Runde, Wirtschaftskammer, Wien, Mai.

Robison, H. David, 1988, Industrial Pollution Abatement: the Impact on Balance of Trade, *Canadian Journal of Economics* 21 (1): 187-199.

Sanchez, Roberto, 1990, Health and Environmental Risks of the Maquiladora in Mexicali, *Natural Resources Journal*, vol. 30, winter 1990.

Schleicher, Stefan, 1991, Konturen für eine neue österreichische Energiepolitik, *Wirtschaftspolititsche Blätter* 2/1991: 155-163.

Schumacher, D., 1988, Regional- und Warenstuktur im internationalen Vergleich, in: DIW (Deutsches Institut für Wirtschaftsforschung)-*Vierteljahreshefte zur Wirtschaftsforschung* 3/4.

Schwarz, Erich, 1994, *Verwertung von Produktionsrückständen durch zwischenbetriebliches Recycling unter besonderer Berücksichtigung der recyclingorientierten zwischenbetrieblichen Kooperation*, dissertation, University of Graz, forthcoming May.

Shrybman, Steven, 1989, *International Trade and the Environment: An Environmental Assessment of Present GATT Negotiations*, Canadian Environmental Law Association.

_____, 1991, Trading Away the Environment, *World Policy Journal*: 93-110.

Siebert, Horst, 1992, *Economics of the Environment*, Berlin: Springer Verlag, third, revised and enlarged edition.

Sloterdijk, Peter, 1989, *Eurotaoismus - Zur Kritik der Politischen Kinetik*, Franfurt am Main: edition suhrkamp 1450, Neue Folge 450.

Sorsa, Piritta, 1992, GATT and Environment, *The World Economy*, vol. 15, no. 1 (January): 115-133.

Steininger, Karl, 1993, Environmental Illusion in the Depletion of Common Property Resources, *Int. J. of Global Energy Issues*, vol. 5, no. 2: 66-75.

_____, 1994, Reconciling Trade and Environment: Towards a Comparative Advantage for Long Term Policy Goals, *Ecological Economics*, Vol. 9: 23-42.

Streißler, Erich W., 1993, Das Problem der Internalisierung, in: König, Heinz, Umweltverträgliches Wirtschaften als Problem von Wissenschaft und Politik, Jahrestagung Oldenburg 1992, *Schriften des Vereins für Socialpolitik*, Neue Folge, Band 224: 87-110.

Subramanian, Arvind, 1992, Trade Measures for Environment: A Nearly Empty Box?, *The World Economy*, vol. 15, no. 1 (January): 135-152.

SUSTAIN (Verein zur Koordination von Forschung über Nachhaltigkeit), 1994, Endbericht des interdisziplinären Forschungsprogramms "Forschungs- und Entwicklungsbedarf für den Übergang zu einer nachhaltigen Wirtschaft in Österreich, Graz: Technische Universität, Institut für Verfahrenstechnik, Juli.

Tichy, Gunther, 1993, Ökonomische Auswirkungen einer Energieabgabe in Österreich, *Wirtschaft und Gesellschaft*, vol. 19(3): 315-327.

Tobey, James A., 1990, The Effects of Domestic Environmental Policies on Patterns of World Trade: An Empirical Test, *Kyklos*, vol. 43: 191-209.

Tobey, James A., 1991, The Impact of Domestic Environmental Policies on International Trade, presented at the Egon Sohmen Conference on "Economic Evolution and Environmental Concerns", Linz, Austria, August.

Tudini, Angelica, 1993, *Trade and Environment: The Issue of Process and Production Methods*, Fondazione ENI Enrico Mattei, Nota di Lavora 7.93, Milano: Fondazione ENI.

Turner, R. Kerry, 1988, Sustainability, Resource Conservation and Pollution Control: An Overview, in: Turner, R. Kerry (ed.), *Sustainable Environmental Management: Principles and Practice*, London: Belhaven: 1-25.

UBA, Umwelt Bundes Amt, 1993, Umweltschutz und Industriestandort - Der Einfluß umweltbezogener Standortfaktoren auf Investitionsentscheidungen, Berichte 1/93. Berlin: Erich Schmidt Verlag.

Uimonen, Peter and John Whalley, 1991, *Trade and Environment*, A Policy Analysis for the Institute for International Economics, Washington, D.C., September, preliminary version; final publication forthcoming fall 1994.

Ulph, Alistair, 1991, The Choice of Environmental Policy Instruments and Strategic International Trade, in (ed.) Pethig, *Conflicts and Cooperation in Managing Environmental Resources*, Berlin: Springer-Verlag: 111-128.

_____, 1992, Environmental Policy, Plant Location and Government Protection, presented to the Conference "The International Dimension of Environmental Policy", Milano: Fondazione Enrico Mattei, October.

_____, 1993, Environmental Policy and Strategic International Trade, presented to the 1993 Annual Conference of the Confederation of European Economic Associations on Environmental Economics, Oxford, March.

Ulph, David, 1992, Strategic Innovation and Environmental Policy, presented to the Conference "The International Dimension of Environmental Policy", Milano: Fondazione Enrico Mattei, October.

U.S. Congress, Office of Technology Assessment, 1980, *Technology and Steel Industry Competitiveness*, Washington, D.C.: Government Printing Office.

_____, 1992, *Trade and Environment: Conflicts and Opportunities*, OTA-BP-ITE-94, Washington, D.C.: U.S. Government Printing Office, May.

Verbruggen, Harmen, 1991, Contours of a Sustainable International Trade System, *Internationale Spectator*, November - xlv-11: 686-691.

Wackernagel, Mathis, and William R. Rees, 1992a, Appropriated Carrying Capacity: Measuring the Natural Requirement of the Human Economy, paper contributed to the Second meeting of the International Society for Ecological Economics, Stockholm, August.

_____, 1992b, Perceptual and Structural Barriers to Investing in Natural Capital, paper contributed to the Second meeting of the International Society for Ecological Economics, Stockholm, August.

Whalley, John and Randall Wigle, 1991, The International Incidence of Carbon Taxes, in: Dornbusch, Rüdiger and James M. Poterba (eds.), *Economic Policy Responses to Global Warming*, Cambridge, MA: MIT Press.

Wießner, Elke, 1991, *Umwelt und Außenhandel* - Der Einbau von Umweltgütern in die komparativ-statische und dynamische Außenwirtschaftstheorie, Nomos, Universitätsschriften Wirtschaft, Baden-Baden.

Wirtschaftskammer Österreich, 1993, Die Ergebnisse der GATT-Uruguay-Runde, Abteilung für Integrations- und Handelspolitik, Wien, mimeo, December.

Wysham, Dapne, 1990, The Codex Connection, Big Business Hijacks GATT, *The Nation*, Dec. 17.

Zarsky, Lyuba, 1991, Trade-Environment Linkages and Sustainable Development, Nautilus Pacific Research Paper, North Fitzroy, Australia, October.

REFERENCES - CGE (Chapter V):

Adelman, Irma and Sherman Robinson, 1978, *Income Distribution Policies in Developing Countries*, Stanford: Stanford University Press.

Armington, Paul S., 1969, A Theory of Demand for Products Distinguished by Place of Production, International Monetary Fund *Staff Papers* 16. Washington D.C.: IMF: 159-178.

Arrow, Kenneth J. and Gerard Debreu, 1954, Existence of an Equilibrium for a Competitive Economy. *Econometrica* 22(3), July: 265-290.

Arrow, Kenneth J., 1959, Towards a Theory of Price Adjustment. In: M. Abramovitz (ed.), *The Allocation of Resources*. Stanford: Stanford University Press.

Auerbach, A. and L. Kotlikoff , 1983, National Savings, Economic Welfare and the Structure of Taxation. In: M. Feldstein (ed.), *Behavioral Simulation Methods in Tax Policy Analysis*. Chicago: University of Chicago Press.

_____, 1987, *Dynamic Fiscal Policy*. Cambridge: Cambridge University Press.

Ballard, C., 1983, Evaluation of the Consumption tax with Dynamic General Equilibrium Models. Ph.D. Dissertation, Stanford University.

Bergman, Lars, 1988, Energy Policy Modeling: A Survey of General Equilibrium Approaches. *Journal of Policy Modeling* 10(3): 377-399.

_____, 1990, The Development of Computable General Equilibrium Modeling. In Bergman, Lars, Dale W. Jorgenson and Erno Zalai, *General Equilibrium Modeling and Economic Policy Analysis*. Cambridge, Mass.: Basil Blackwell.

_____, 1991, General Equilibrium Effects of Environmental Policy: A CGE-Modeling Approach. *Environmental and Resource Economics* 1:43-61.

_____, 1993, General Equilibrium Costs and Benefits of Environmental Policies: Some Preliminary Results Based on Swedish Data. Presented to the Confederation of European Economic Associations Conference on Environmental Economics, Oxford, March.

Boyd, Roy and Kerry Krutilla, 1992, Controlling Acid Deposition: A General Equilibrium Assessment. *Environmental and Resource Economics* 2:307-322.

Brendemoen, Anne and Haakon Vennemo, 1992, A Climate Convention and the Norwegian Economy: A CGE Assessment. Central Bureau of Statistics, Oslo, mimeo.

Breuss, Fritz and Jean Tesche, 1991, A CGE Model of Austria, Some Implications of Trade Liberalization. *Empirica* (18:2): 135-165.

Brooke, Anthony, David Kendrick and Alexander Meeraus, 1988, *GAMS - A User´s Guide* (Release 2.25: 1992). The Scientific Press: South San Francisco, California.

Bundesministerium für Umwelt, 1993, *Ökonomisch-Ökologische Modellbildung*, Kommentierte Literaturübersicht und Anwendungskonzepte für Österreich, Schriftenreihe der Sektion I, Band 2/1993, Autoren: Stephan Fickl, Peter Fleissner, Heidi Grundwald, Wolfgang Hofkirchner, Andrea Höltl, Klemens Leutgöb, Manfred Mühlberger, Margit Pohl, Karl Steininger und Anton Steurer. Wien, April.

Burniaux, J. M., J. P. Martin, G. Nicoletti and J. Oliveira-Martins, 1991, GREEN - A Multi-Region Dynamic General Equilibrium Model for Quantifying the Costs of Curbing CO2 Emissions: A technical Manual, OECD, Department of Economics and Statistics Working Paper 89. Paris: OECD.

_____, 1992, The Costs of Reducing CO2 Emissions: Evidence from GREEN, OECD, Economics Department Working Paper 115. Paris: OECD.

Capros, Pantelis, 1992, The SOLFEGE/GEM-E-3 Computable General Equilibrium Approach in Modeling Economy-Energy-Environment Interactions for Europe, presented to the Conference on Modeling Economy-Environment Linkages, Fondazione ENI Enrico Mattei, Milano, December.

Devarajan, Shanta, 1988, Natural Resources and Taxation in Computable General Equilibrium Models of Developing Countries. *Journal of Policy Modeling* 10(4): 505-528.

_____, 1990, Can Computable General Equilibrium Models Shed Light on the Environmental Problems of Developing Countries? John F. Kennedy School of Government, Harvard University, mimeo.

Dixon, Peter B., B.R. Parmenter, J. Sutton and D.P. Vincent, 1982, *ORANI: A Multisectoral Model of the Australian Economy.* Amsterdam: North-Holland.

Dervis, K., 1975, Substitution, Employment and Intertemporal Equilibrium in a Non-Linear Multi-Sector Planning Model of Turkey. *European Economic Review*, vol. 6: 77-96.

Drud, Arne Stolbjerg, 1992, GAMS/CONOPT, Appendix to the GAMS User´s Guide. Arki Consulting: Bagsvaerd, Denmark.

Dungan, P.D., 1980, An Empirical, Multi-Sectoral Walrasian-keynesian Model of the Canadian Economy. Ph.D. Dissertation, Princeton University.

Farmer, Karl and Karl Steininger, 1994, Sustainable Air Quality and Sectorial Production in an Intertemporal CGE-Model of Austria, Conference Proceedings: Models of Sustainable Development, Paris: Université Panthéon-Sorbonne: 281-292.

Forrester, J.W., 1986, *Principles of Systems*, MIT Press, Cambridge, Mass.

_____, 1972, *Collected Papers*, MIT Press, Cambridge, Mass.

Ginsburgh, V.A. and Jean L. Waelbroeck, 1981, *Activity Analysis and General Equilibrium Modeling*. Amsterdam: North-Holland.

Glomsrod, Solveig, Haakon Vennemo and Torgeir Johnsen, 1991, Stabilization of Emissions of CO_2: A Computable General Equilibrium Assessment. Central Bureau of Statistics, Oslo.

Goreux, L.M. and A.S. Manne (eds.), 1973, *Multi-level Planning: Case Studies in Mexico*. Amsterdam: North-Holland.

Hazilla, Michael and Raymond J. Kopp, 1990, Social Cost of Environmental Quality Regulations: A General Equilibrium Analysis, *Journal of Political Economy*, 98(4): 853-873.

Hinojosa-Ojeda, Raul, Sherman Robinson and Jean Tesche, 1992, Hungary, Austria and the European Community: A CGE Model of Economic Reform and Integration, University of California, Berkeley, Department of Agriculture and Resource Economics, mimeo.

Hofer,, Markus, 1993, *Instrumente zur Reduktion der Kohlendioxid-Emissionen*, Grazer Schriftenreihe für Verfahrenstechnik 5, Graz: dbv-Verlag für die Technische Universität Graz.

Hudson, E.A. and Dale W. Jorgenson, 1975, US Energy and Economic Growth 1975-2000. *Bell Journal of Economics and Management Science*, 5(2) Autumn: 461-514.

Johansen, Leif , 1960, *A Multi-Sectoral Study of Economic Growth*. Amsterdam: North-Holland.

Jorgenson, Dale W. and Peter J. Wilcoxen, 1990, Intertemporal General Equlibrium Modeling of U.S. Environmental Policy. *Journal of Policy Modeling* 12(4): 715-744.

Keuschnigg, Christian and Wilhelm Kohler, 1993, Dynamic Effects of Tariff Liberalization: An Intertemporal CGE Approach. Institute for Advanced Studies, Vienna, Research Memorandum 315, February.

Lager, Christian, 1993, Ein dynamisches Input-Output-Modell zur Beurteilung fiskalpolitischer Maßnahmen, Diss., Universität Graz.

Leontief, Wassily, 1970, Environmental Repercussions and the Economic Structure: An Input-Output Approach. *Review of Economics and Statistics* 52: 262-271.

Meadows, D.H., D.L. Meadows, J. Randers, W.W. Behrens, 1972, *The Limits to Growth*, London.

Meadows, D.H. and D.L. Meadows, 1992, *The New Limits to Growth*, London.

Nestor, Deborah V. and Carl A. Pasurka, 1992, General Equilibrium Model of German Environmental Regulation, U.S. Environmental Protection Agency, Economic Analysis and Research Branch, Washington, mimeo, March.

_____, 1993a, Welfare Effects of Environmental Control: The German Example, U.S. Environmental Protection Agency, Economic Analysis and Research Branch, Washington, mimeo, April.

_____, 1993b, Environment-Economic Accounting and Indicators of the Economic Importance of Environmental Protection Activities, U.S. Environmental Protection Agency, Economic Analysis and Research Branch, Washington, mimeo, September.

Nicoletti, Giuseppe, 1990, Green Project - Survey of Interfactor and Interenergy Elasticities. Paris: OECD, mimeo, November 15.

ÖSTAT, Österreichisches Statistisches Zentralamt, Energieausstoß und -einsatz der Österreichischen Volkswirtschaft im Jahre 1974, *Statistische Nachrichten*, 31. Jhg., Heft 7: 499-506.

_____, 1990, Energieversorgung Österreichs, Jahresheft 1989, Wien.

_____, 1991, Energieversorgung Österreichs, Jahresheft 1990, Wien.

_____, 1992a, Energieversorgung Österreichs, Jahresheft 1991, Wien.

_____, 1992b, Monetäre Aufwendungen für den Energetischen Endverbrauch im Jahr 1988, *Statistische Nachrichten*, 47. Jhg., Heft 12: 1027-1035.

_____, 1992c, Energieaufbringung und -verwendung in der Österreichischen Volkswirtschaft im Jahr 1989 - Endgültige Energiebilanz 1989, *Statistische Nachrichten*, 47. Jhg., Heft 6: 490-506.

_____, 1993, Statistische Übersichten, monthly supplement to *Statistische Nachrichten* and Austrian Institute of Economic Research, *Monatsberichte*, Wien.

Pereira, Alfredo M. and John B. Shoven, 1988, Survey of Dynamic Computational General Equilibrium Models for Tax Policy Analysis. *Journal of Policy Modeling* 10(3): 401-436.

Pezzey, John, 1991, Analysis of Unilateral Carbon Taxes Using the Whalley-Wigle Global Energy Model, presented to the Annual Meeting of the European Association of Environmental and Resource Economists, Stockholm, June.

Piggot, John, John Whalley and Randall Wigle, 1991, How Large are the Incentives to Join Sub-Global Carbon Reduction Initiatives?. University of New South Wales, Sydney, mimeo.

Piggot, John and John Whalley, 1992, *Economic Impacts of Carbon Reduction Schemes: Some General Equilibrium Estimates from a Simple Global Model.* Working Paper Series No. 17, Center for Economic Studies, University of Munich, June.

Poterba, Jaames M., 1991, Tax Policy to Combat Global Warming: On Designing a Carbon Tax. In: Dornbusch, Rudiger and James Poterba, *Global Warming: Economic Policy Responses*, MIT Press.

Robinson, Sherman, 1990, Pollution, Market Failure, and Optimal Policy in an Economywide Framework. University of California at Berkeley, Department of Agricultural and Resource Economics: Working Paper No 559.

Robinson, Sherman, Shankar Subramanian and Jacqueline Geoghegan, 1994, Modeling Air Pollution Abatement in a Market Based Incentive Framework for the Los Angeles Basin. In: Foresund, Finn and Ger Klaassen, *Economic Instruments for Air Pollution Control*, Kluwer (in press).

Rutherford, Thomas, 1988, *General Equilibrium Modeling with MPS/GE*. University of Western Ontario, London, Ontario.

Schleicher, Stefan P., 1992, Rethinking the Use of Energy Elasticities, presented to the Workshop on Estimating Long-Run Energy Elasticities, Cambridge, September.

Schröder, Michael, 1990, *Die Volkswirtschaftlichen Kosten von Umweltpolitik*. Kosten-Wirksamkeitsanalysen mit einem Angewandten Allgemeinen Gleichgewichtsmodell. Heidelberg: Physica-Verlag.

Shoven, John B. and John Whalley, 1984, Applied General Equilibrium Models of Taxation and Trade: An Introduction and Survey. *Journal of Economic Literature*, vol. XXII (September): 1007-1051.

_____, 1992, *Applying General Equilibrium*. Cambridge: Cambridge University Press.

Shoven, John B., John Whalley and Wolfgang Wiegard, 1992, Computing General Equilibria. In: Shoven, J.B. and J. Whalley, *Applying General Equilibrium*. Cambridge: Cambridge University Press.

South Coast Air Quality Management District, 1993, *RECLAIM: The Regional Clean Air Incentives Market: Final Volume 1*. Diamond Bar, CA, October.

Stephan, Gunter, Renger van Nieuwkoop and Thomas Wiedmer, 1992, Social Incidence and Economic Costs of Carbon Limits: A Computable General Equilibrium Analysis for Switzerland. University of Berne, Institute for Applied Microeconomics, mimeo.

Takayama, T. and G. C. Judge, 1971, *Spatial and Temporal Price and Allocation Models*. Amsterdam: North-Holland.

Taylor, Lance, 1975, Theoretical Foundations and Technical Implications, in: Blitzer, Charles R., Peter B. Clark and Lance Taylor (ed.), *Economy-Wide Models and Development Planning*. Published for the World Bank, London: Oxford University Press.

UBA, Umweltbundesamt, 1992, CO_2-Emmissionsentwicklung und Prognose für Österreich, Berechnungen bis 2005 auf Grundlage der Energieprognose des WIFO vom Dezember 1991, Wien.

Wald, Abraham, 1934, Über die Eindeutige Positive Lösbarkeit der Neuen Produktionsgleichungen. *Ergebnisse eines Mathematischen Kolloquiums*, Band 6, 1933-1934, Wien.

GPSR Compliance

The European Union's (EU) General Product Safety Regulation (GPSR) is a set of rules that requires consumer products to be safe and our obligations to ensure this.

If you have any concerns about our products, you can contact us on ProductSafety@springernature.com

In case Publisher is established outside the EU, the EU authorized representative is:

Springer Nature Customer Service Center GmbH
Europaplatz 3
69115 Heidelberg, Germany

Batch number: 10725979

Printed by Printforce, the Netherlands